THIS BOOK IS A MUST-READ FOR ...

... the professional feeling slightly stuck in coping with the challenges the fast-changing world throws at him.

... the change manager, professional or agent driven to spread a culture of change within his organisation.

... the leader searching to create an engaged team of people that dare to take initiatives and think outside the box.

... everyone looking for the tools, the language and the energy to boost their creative and entrepreneurial mindset.

CONTENT

Concept & Content
Cyriel Kortleven

Illustrations
Cyriel Kortleven

Graphic design
Kathleen Steegmans
Mistimages.be

Text editors
David Esterhuysen
Katrien De Cannière

ISBN: 9789082935004
First printed October 2018

Bookazine published in collaboration with
Passionpreneur Publishing

WWW.CYRIELKORTLEVEN.COM

CONTENT

88
SWITCHING PERSPECTIVE

Hi there!

Thank you for buying and reading this bookazine. I hope that I can inspire you with some new tools, language and energy to boost your Change Mindset. But before we set off on that journey, I have a few more gifts to offer you because I truly am grateful that you take the time and energy to read my bookazine.

Free digital access of this bookazine

To improve your reading experience, you can access the digital version of the bookazine for free (it's only for free for the people who bought the hardcopy). It is meant as an addition to the bookazine, so I will ask you not to spread it in your network.
Visit www.changemindsetbook.com and answer a simple question to access to the digital version.

Discount access 'Online Global Change Mindset Summit'

At the beginning of 2019, I will be launching an online Global Change Mindset Summit with more than 25 interviews with experts from all over the world on the topic of the Change Mindset. You'll find excerpts of some of those interviews integrated in this bookazine where relevant. But there's more to them. The extensive interviews will be put online next year. Having purchased this bookazine will allow for a discount access to the extended content.

Extra cool 'stuff' inspiration

When you terminate reading the bookazine and you actually do find the tips, tricks and tools usefull; you might be interested in downloading the poster with ideakillers, ideaboosters, the Yes And Act manifesto, cartoons. You can access them via the link below. Feel free to use these materials for your own purpose and help spreading the Change Mindset.
Check out https://www.cyrielkortleven.com/downloadcoolstuff/

Donation 10% to charity 'Together We Can Change The World'

I'm joining a global speaking tour with the fantastic team of 'Together We Can Change The World'. This association is dedicated to improving the well-being of disadvantaged children and women in South East Asia. We offer both funding and our professional skills to carefully vetted organisations that provide education and job-skills training to these people enabling them to achieve independent, self-sustaining lives. I will be spending two weeks in the Philippines in 2019 with the TWCCTW crew. 10% of all revenues from this bookazine will be donated to TWCCTW which means that you have already done a good deed by buying this book.
Feel free to make an extra donation to this charity: www.twcctw.org

Stay in touch

It would be wonderful to stay connected. I deliver keynotes all over the world and off course I would relish any opportunity to collaborate with your organisation. I send out max 5 inspiration newsletters a year to keep my tribe updated on new content, tools, ... around the Change Mindset. If you want to keep your fire going, do subscribe for the newsletter or blog on www.cyrielkortleven.com/contact or connect with me on Linkedin.

TSUNDOKU

I designed this 'bookazine' so as to avoid the trap of 'Tsundoku'. Tsundoku is the term used for acquiring reading materials, but letting them pile up in one's home without reading them- typically found on shelves, floors and nightstands. I believe that too many interesting books have been created with far too little attention spent on the design and layout.

You may argue that 'Content is King', but there has been a kind of evolution in the speaking business centered around the idea that 'Experience is Queen'. As we all know, it is she who runs the household. Few people enjoy listening to a boring speaker even if they have brilliant content to offer. Of course, the content should be top-quality, but I'm quite sure that audiences the world over will capture far more of the content if the 'experience' around it is outstanding. You will find this deeply stimulating theme of 'Yes, and'- thinking (instead of the well-known and horrifyingly demotivating 'Yes, but ...' phrase) in this book, so bear with me in my attempt to achieve great content AND a great experience.

The writing process of this bookazine has been a very interesting journey. I have explored many sidetracks and gathered a lot more input than necessary; but I find less is beautiful. I see myself more as a curator and simplifier instead of claiming thought-leadership, and so you will find a lot of references to great thinkers and doers in this bookazine. My goal was to prevent you from spending too much time researching and evaluating top-quality content. I set out to do that task for you, and to present it to you a condensed version so as to allow you to enjoy the best insights out there in an agreeable and time-efficient way. I serve this to you with an inspiring sauce of humour and practical tools. At least, I am already pleased with the result and I do hope you will enjoy the content as well as the reading experience.

Cyriel Kortleven

A CHANGI

When the world goes bananas ...

The VUCA rhythm - volatile, uncertain, complex and ambiguous - has taken over the world. Yesterday has come to pass. Facts and figures prove that change is the only constant. New professions come into existence, shaping future opportunities.

NG WORLD

THE WORLD OF YESTERDAY

THE W
TO

REACTIVE

PROTECT INFORMATION

SINGLE
SOLUTION

SOLVING
PROBLEMS

REALISTIC DREAMS

CONTROL

PLANNING

REDUCING RISKS

STABILITY

NEED

RIGHT SKILLS

PREDICT FUTURE

NO MISTAKES

EXPERTS IN ONE INDUSTRY

RELAX. EVERYTHING IS
UNDER CONTROL.

We cur
world of ec
disruptive technolc
competitors who are figh
of ever more demanding cus

Volatility. Challenges are
be of unknown durati
turbulence c

Uncertainty. The lack of predictabi
sense of awareness and understandi
a worldwhere it is very hard

Complexity. The multiplex of forces
that surrounds organisations. We
inter-connected, anc

Ambiguity. The hazines
cause-and-effect confu
where nobody has
anyn

A CHANG

RLD OF
AY

ve in a
turbulence,
alisation and a lot of
h other to fulfill the needs
We live in a VUCA world.

cted or unstable and may
're living in a world full of
at instability.

prospects for surprise and the
sues and events. We're living in
dict the direction of the future.

THE WORLD OF TOMORROW

PROACTIVE

SHARE & LEARN

A VARIETY OF
SOLUTIONS

EXPLORING
OPPORTUNITIES

DISRUPTIVE DREAMS

TRUST

EXPERIMENT

MOTION

AGILITY

thechangemindset.video/pendulum

SINGLE OR DOUBLE?

In this movie, you'll see the difference between a single and a double pendulum. It's a great metaphor to illustrate the difference between the world of yesterday (a single pendulum) and tomorrow (a double pendulum).

Inspired by Peter Hinssen
Movie created by Ami Versano

1 in 4 People Hate Their Job

A study by Gallup found that only 13% of employees feel engaged by their jobs. 'Engaged' means that they feel a sense of passion for their work, a deep connection to their employer and they spend their days driving innovation as well as moving their company forward.

The vast majority (around 63%) are 'not engaged', meaning that they are unhappy, but not drastically so. In short, they have checked out. They sleepwalk through their days, putting little energy into their work.

A full 24% are what Gallup calls 'actively disengaged'- meaning that they pretty much hate their jobs. They act out, and actually undermine what their coworkers accomplish.

Furthermore, I was shocked to learn that 87% of the workers worldwide are emotionally disconnected from their workplaces and are not fulfilling their full professional potential.

* Gallup - Worldwide employee study (> 200,000 respondents) between 2011-2012.

Major Barrier to Success: Changing Mindset and Attitude

A study from IBM 10 years ago (but still relevant today) around the success / failure rates of "change" projects finds:

- Only 40% of projects met the schedule, budget and quality goals
- The best organizations are 10 times more successful than inferior organisations
- The biggest barriers to success listed as people factors: changing mindsets and attitudes – 58%. Corporate culture – 49%. Lack of senior management support – 32%.
- Underestimation of complexity listed as a factor in 35% of projects

* IBM study, 1500 change management executives, 2008

Delivering a Happiness Shock Increased Productivity

Researchers randomly chose 700 individuals and either showed them a 10-minute comedy clip or provided them with snacks and drinks. They then followed up with a series of questions to ensure that the "happiness shocks" (as they're referred to in the report), actually made the subjects happy. When it was confirmed that they did, the researchers gave them tasks to measure their levels of productivity.

The experiment showed that productivity increased by an average of 12% and reached as high as 20% above the control group. By way of comparison, Dr. Daniel Sgroi, the author of the report, noted that with regard to GDP and economic growth, rises of 3% or so are considered very large.

* Social Market Foundation and the University of Warwick's Centre for Competitive Advantage in the Global Economy, a study in October 2015.

FACTS & FIGURES

Change is the Only Constant

96% of organisations today are in some phase of transformation (*1), and nearly half have completed at least one transformation in the last 23 months (*2).

*(*1) The Decision Driven Organization. Blenko, Mankins and Rogers. HBR, 2010.*
*(*2) Surviving in Disruptive Times: KMPG Global Transformation Study, 2016.*

Happy is productive

A study by economists at the University of Warwick found that happiness led to a 12% peak in productivity, while unhappy workers proved 10% less productive.

* University of Warwick – Happiness of Employees, 2014.

Complexity Rules

A study on complexity by the Boston Consulting Group shows that since 1955, organisational complexity has gone up 6-fold, whilst the number of procedures and rules to fight the same complexity has seen a 35-fold increase!

In the more complicated organisations, managers spend:

more than 40% of their time writing reports and between 30 – 60% of their time on (coordination) meetings.

The logical question that follows is, when do they get actual work done? Or do we consider 'managing' as synonymous with writing reports and coordinating other people's tasks?

* Smart Rules: Six Ways to Get People to Solve Problems Without You - Boston Consulting Group. 2014.

PROFESSIONS OF TOMORROW

* ## Alternative Currency Speculator

Digital currencies are on the rise as people lose trust in government-controlled currencies. To help you ensure that you do not have a failed financial credit in the future, you will need a digital currency advisor who understands cryptocurrencies. This will help to balance a diversified digital portfolio.

* ## Productivity Counselor

With the emphasis on productivity and 'work-life-balance', coupled with new tracking devices, employees will need help refining their lives to improve their productivity- combining ergonomics, wellness, time management and career counseling.

* ## Food Engineer

3D printing has taken the world by storm. From simple uses like creating models in the cosmetics industry, to more complicated arenas like prosthetics, 3D printing continues to develop. In the near future, there will be 3D food printing using the same technology as 3D printing, but creating different types of food, some of which will be edible.

* ## End of Life Therapist

As life spans increase, planning for the last phases of life will become standard practice. End of life therapists will act as guides to planning the years before a client's death. This will involve being straight-forward, but sensitive about ways to make dying a smoother process. They will collaborate with a Digital Death Manager who will create, manage or eliminate content to craft one's online presence posthumously.

EVERYTHING IS RELATIVE

"Everything is now ultra, in thinking and in doing. We don't know ourselves anymore; we don't understand the element in which we exist and are active ... Young people are aroused and then swept into the contemporary whirlpool. The world admires wealth and speed, and everyone strives for both."

Johann Wolfgang von Goethe (1749 - 1832) mentions the effect of the railroad, express mail, steamships, and other methods of modern communication. Letter Goethe to 1825 to Zelter

"THE STONE AGE DIDN'T END BECAUSE THEY RAN OUT OF STONES."

ANONYMOUS

* Virtual Reality Architect

The combination of virtual reality and artificial intelligence leads to many new applications. Companies like IKEA are already embracing these technologies to show the 3D full-size products via their catalogue app on the tablets and phones of their potential clients.

* Digital detox therapist

A counselor who specialises in separating technology-stressed individuals from their devices, creating unique analog immersion zones.

* 'Rewilder'

Natural landscapes continue to disappear across the globe as a result of overdevelopment, natural disaster and industrial farming. Therefore, it will be critical in the future to have a fleet of rewilders who have agricultural and wildlife management training to return nature to some of the environment's most forsaken locations.

* Organ Harvester

There are currently several labs around the world that can grow human organs in a simple petri dish. Eventually, this technology will become commercially available and there will be a need for an organ harvester to plant and then harvest the organs prior to them being implanted by robot-surgeons.

* Media Remixer

A media remixer takes the job of DJ or VJ to another level by remixing various forms of media into one cohesive new project. These remixers will bring together audio, video, images and augmented reality to create projects ranging from marketing campaigns, wedding entertainment to installation art.

* Commercial Civilian Drone Operators

With the continued popularity of drones, in the future there will be drones for almost everything including delivery services, forensics and filming. Once drones have rightfully taken up an essential place in the world there will be a great need for commercial civilian drone operators. This will require a pilot's license and additional extensive training and experience.

ANGELO VERMEULEN

SPACE SYSTEMS RESEARCHER, BIOLOGIST, ARTIST, KEYNOTE SPEAKER, DELFT UNIVERSITY OF TECHNOLOGY, BIOMODD, SEAD (SPACE ECOLOGIES ART AND DESIGN), ECOLOGY, TECHNOLOGY, COMMUNITY, GLOBAL NETWORK, CREW COMMANDER NASA-FUNDED HI-SEAS MARS SIMULATION, SENIOR TED FELLOW.

LET THE END RESULT EMERGE

"During our community art project 'Biomodd' we recycle e-waste and build functioning networks with the different computer components. We then create a living ecosystem inside the computer network that uses the waste heat of the electronics. Together with fellow collaborators of the SEAD collective, we've created Biomodd projects all over the world, and every single project version involves a new group of participants. We always start with the same core idea: e-waste, recycling, and the integration of living biology. The end result can differ widely, depending on the kind of community we're working with. We start with a few guiding principles, but the result emerges out of the local group and is certainly not fixed at the start of the project.

It's crucial to find the right balance between a goal that's not too abstract, and one that's not too specific either. If it's too open-ended, people lose their sense of direction and consequently lose their motivation. If the goal is too specific, people will also disconnect because they don't want to feel like a robot simply executing orders. The right balance will lead to a situation where people feel involved and engaged because there is room for their ideas, and they feel the contribution they make is actually meaningful. It's the task of a good leader to play around with this 'slider,' moving between complete openness at one side of the spectrum, and a detailed blueprint with pre-planned tasks at the other side."

Profile picture © Wim Van Eesbeek
Other pictures © Angelo Vermeulen

AN AGILE MINDSET

"Freedom and responsibility go hand in hand, and people will respond differently to these. Some people feel more secure when things are predefined by a leader, while others prefer to have more responsibility and want to try out new things on their own. You can explore this by inviting people to experiment and take up way more responsibility than what they're used to. Of course, the feasibility of such an approach depends on the type of projects and departments people are involved in.

I would start experimenting with a more loose leadership style in a department where the organization needs a lot of innovation. Start there, and it might radiate to other departments. And it doesn't mean that it's a bad strategy if there are a few failures. Failures are a crucial part of the agile mindset. Also, make sure that you are sensitive about both the group dynamics and the individual needs of people. You can't apply an agile mindset just by reading a manual. There's a craft to develop and apply an agile mindset."

SWITCH LEADERSHIP ROLES FOR A WEEK

"In the HI-SEAS project, a NASA-funded Mars mission simulation, the main objective is to investigate the psychological effect of long-term isolation on small crews. During the first HI-SEAS mission, I was the commander of a crew of five, living for four months on the slope of the Mauna Loa volcano in Hawaii (resembling the Martian surface).

One of the things I found quite important was having short morning and evening meetings where everybody would speak up and share what was on their mind. Some crew members had questions about the necessity of such sharing and preferred to focus on the operational side of the mission. Out of curiosity, I asked the crew who was actually interested in leading the mission, and four out of five people raised their hands. I accepted the challenge and turned this situation into a small social experiment. For the next four weeks, different crew members took turns acting as crew commander. And at the end of every week, we had an open evaluation of each experience. One major advantage of the experiment was the fact that my colleagues could understand better what it's like to be the leader in such a situation.

However, sometimes it was also quite painful to hear that certain new ways of working were actually perceived to be better than my own carefully crafted method. At those moments, you have to put your ego to the side, and learn from the experience. In the end, it was a very interesting learning curve for all of us."

LADDERS &

Human beings love to think in patterns. Which is great, otherwise we wouldn't even survive. However, if we always stick to the things we already know (our inherent aversion to change would advise us to do so) - it can lead to feeling profoundly stuck both on a personal level - a world plastered and limited by assumptions - as well as on an organisational level, commonly referred to as bureaucracy.

In this chapter we explore the 'ladder & banana'-metaphor and its consequences to depict just how utterly stuck we tend to get...

BANANAS

THOUGHT PATTERNS IN OUR BRAIN

The book 'Creativity in Business' written by Igor Byttebier and Ramon Vullings explains that human beings are constantly surrounded by all kind of stimuli. Via our perception systems (senses), we can capture these stimuli. In our brain these stimuli are 'translated', and reactions are triggered. Our thinking can be defined as the processing of that information. Thought patterns are clusters of data that we recognize as clusters, that we will store if and when they generate success. In a comparable situation, we can quickly retrieve these patterns and apply them again. Eventually this occurs automatically, so we can focus our attention on new or more important problems. These thought patterns are the habits of our thinking. We can therefore define experience as the sum of all patterns and habits we have acquired.

Logical thinking is a system that works well most of the time (e.g. walking, talking, brushing your teeth, driving a car and most activities at work are repetitive tasks). It is therefore quite logical that a thought system which derives its strength from stability of patterns and habits will encounter some difficulties when required to break these patterns and habits. That is (understandably) the main reason why we find pattern-breaking thinking or creative thinking quite hard.

There is absolutely nothing wrong with habits. We've needed them for survival in ancient times, as we do now. That being said, in some cases (like environmental changes, which occur quite frequently) it would be useful if our patterns easily adapted to the new situation. Unfortunately, more often than not that is not the case- so we are stuck with old thinking patterns that block real change and progress.

Daniel Kahneman explains in his book 'Thinking Fast and Slow' that we have two distinct brain systems that help us reason and produce different results. System 1 (gut, a brilliant device) works instantaneously without you being conscious of it. You use it when you feel intuitively that something is wrong or right, without knowing or reasoning out exactly why.

System 1 operates based on a few simple rules. The law of similarity is one of them. If something looks like a snake, it probably is a snake and you should run away as fast as possible. Though you can imagine a situation where that would be useful, I believe you will admit that it isn't flawless. System 1 is often inaccurate and does not adapt well to new situations.

System 2 (mind, an equally stunning asset) runs on conscious thought and it is at its best when you carefully think over a problem or situation. However, system 2 has 2 major disadvantages: it is slow, and it needs to be trained to react in the right way to any given situation.

You can imagine that system 1 often plays an important role in new situations to 'protect' ourselves. In the context of system 1, every change is by definition a danger. This is precisely what makes a lot of change projects so hard to realise.

Creativity in Business by Igor Byttebier and Ramon Vullings

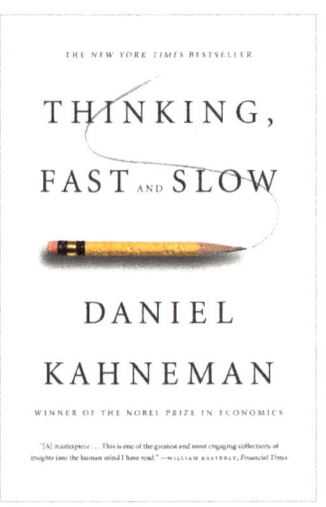

Thinking fast and slow by Daniel Kahneman

"OUT OF THE BOX OR OUT OF BUSINESS."

CYRIEL KORTLEVEN

STUCK ON AN ESCALATOR

thechangemindset.video/brokenescalator

There's a brilliant movie - a commercial for Becel from Tim Piper - where two business people are stuck on an escalator. Due to a malfunction, the escalator comes to a stop. The two people stand still and continue to do so for a period of time-eventually getting frustrated and even calling out for help. For the sake of humour, neither one of them seems to grasp the possibility of using the escalator as an ordinary staircase.

Walking up the escalator would adequately solve their predicament. We would naturally compliment ourselves on having slightly more wit then these characters, feeling sure this wouldn't happen to us. Or would it? If you really think about it, in how many situations have you felt like you were stuck on that escalator? How often do you feel 'forced' to accept the status quo because there is no budget, because a certain solution (once upon a time) has already been tried, or because the market is supposedly not ready yet? In reality, we constantly allow ourselves to be fooled by these excuses.

EXERCISE 1

Think fast: A bat and ball cost $1.10, and the bat costs one dollar more than the ball. How much does the ball cost?

Did you think the answer was $0.10? If you take a second and do the math, you'll see that the correct answer is $0.05. But don't feel bad – almost everyone makes this mistake at first!

EXERCISE 2

Connect the 9 dots with 4 straight lines.

A smartass, are you? Then try connecting all dots with 1 line and find at least 3 alternative solutions for this challenge.

You literally have to think out of the box to solve this problem. The puzzle only seems difficult because people usually imagine a boundary around the edge of the dotted area. In fact, it is even possible to connect all dots with one line if you allow creativity to step out of your own assumptions. You could use a very thick marker; or fold the paper in a way that all dots are lined up and put a pencil through them. Furthermore, using some origami techniques will also help to solve this challenge. If you find any other other solutions, feel free to send an email to me with your solution.

EXERCISE 3

Count the Fs in the sentence below.

FINISHED FILES ARE THE
RESULT OF YEARS OF
SCIENTIFIC STUDY
COMBINED WITH THE
EXPERIENCE OF YEARS.

Did you count 3? or 4? There are actually 6 F's in this sentence. Out-of-the-box-thinkers can even spot more. With a little bit of imagination, you can discover an F in every E. If has one line too many, but what does that mean the F is not in there? What is blocking your imagination?

BRAINTEASERS

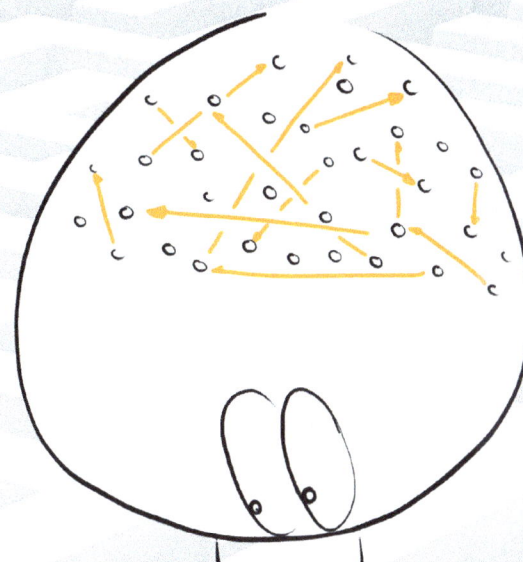

EXERCISE 4

Can you answer all questions correctly?

1. Johnny's mother has three children. The first child was named April. The second child was named May. What is the third child called?

2. Before Mount Everest was discovered what was the highest mountain in the world?

3. Billie was born on December 28th, yet her birthday always falls in the summer. How is this possible?

4. In British Columbia, you cannot take a picture of a man with a wooden leg. Why not?

5. If you were running a race and you passed the person in 2nd place, what place would you be in now?

5. You would be in 2nd place. You passed the person in second place, not first.
4. You can't take a picture with a wooden leg. You need a camera (or smart-phone) to take a picture.
3. Billie lives on the Southern hemisphere.
2. Mount Everest. It just wasn't discovered yet.
1. Johnny

EXERCISE 5

Which one is the odd one out?

You can probably argue that they are all odd, but the most 'special' one is the most 'common' one and that's the first symbol (red square with border). It has the most common characteristics - there are 4 elements that are red and have borders. It's the only one that isn't the odd one out, which makes it unique.

THE DIFFERENT SHAPES OF FEARS

Sometimes, the acronym False Expectations Appearing Real is used to describe fear. This means that a lot of the fears that we have are not real. They only exist in our mind. Other fears have something to do with the inevitable -like death, for example. At that moment we try to ignore the subject, deny it or get morbidly obsessed by it, pondering about the meaninglessness of life. However, at this very moment we can't do anything about dying, so it is almost bizarre that death itself is feared so fiercely. It is one of the few certainties in life. A realistic fear would be to die unprepared, or to feel that we haven't lived to our full potential. This fear can stimulate us to take action at this moment to make sure that we do have a meaningful life.

Of course, we have many fears. We're afraid of the unknown, of change, of conflict, of vulnerability, of failure, of not being good enough, of loneliness, of being incompetent, of criticism, of responsibility, of pain and ... well, the list goes on and on. On some idle day, I once counted the number of 'phobias' on Wikipedia and found that there are 120 different fears attested to there. There are

the well-known variants like arachnophobia (fear of spiders) or claustrophobia (fear of having no escape and being closed in), but there are also a few bizarre ones:

Aichmophobia (fear of sharp or pointed objects), Coulrophobia (fear of clowns) and my favorite one Hexakosioihexekontahexaphobia - fear of the number 666. I'm also quite sure you don't want to suffer from Phonophobia - fear of having a phobia.

You can bring most fears back to one root: that we won't be able to cope with the challenges life throws at us. If you can establish a deep-rooted trust in your ability to overcome any challenge that life might present you with, your life will become a lot easier. Sometimes, when you face a new situation, you just have to push through your fear to discover it wasn't that 'scary' after all. Studies have shown that only ten percent of what we worry about actually transpires. This means that most of our worries are completely unfounded. I invite you to take into account and acknowledge that we are currently living in humanity's most prosperous time.

As stated before, our biggest fear is probably failing to live to our full potential. The poem from Marianne Williamson describes it in a beautiful way:

"Our deepest fear is not that we are inadequate. Our deepest fear is that we are powerful beyond measure. It is our light, not our darkness that most frightens us. We ask ourselves, Who am I to be brilliant, gorgeous, talented, fabulous? Actually, who are you not to be? You are a child of God. Your playing small does not serve the world. There is nothing enlightened about shrinking so that other people won't feel insecure around you. We are all meant to shine, as children do. We were born to make manifest the glory of God that is within us. It's not just in some of us; it's in everyone. And as we let our own light shine, we unconsciously give other people permission to do the same. As we are liberated from our own fear, our presence automatically liberates others."

A Return to Love
Reflections on the Principles of a Course in Miracles by Marianne Williamson

"The greatest mistake you can make in life is to be continually fearing you will make one."

Elbert Hubbard

There are three kinds of fears that often pop up when we talk about change:

Fear of the Unknown
Being afraid because you don't know what will happen. It makes you want to stick to the status quo even though you know full well that there are some disadvantages to that situation. As the expression rightfully puts it: better the devil you know (than the devil you don't).

Fear of Different Opinions
Being afraid that someone else's opinion doesn't align with your view of the world, so you try to ignore them by sticking to your own perspective.

Fear of Failure
Being afraid that something might go wrong. It makes you overexert yourself in building control mechanisms to make sure that everything turns out as planned. Needless to say, that control is an illusion and things have a habit of turning out differently anyway.

LADDERS & BANANAS

Placing a ladder over a banana peel to avoid people slipping on it is not the most efficient solution. However, if you look at organisations (certainly the bigger ones), it is strange that they have built so many ladders into their structures and systems.

A 'ladder' in this context is used to indicate an inefficient pattern that we keep repeating because it has proven successful in the past, although it currently isn't very efficient or doesn't lead to the results that we want. It could be a procedure that we've installed 10 years ago to solve a certain problem, and although that situation doesn't occur anymore, the procedure is still in place. I will share many examples of 'ladders' in this bookazine, but here are a few common ladders that most professionals recognise.

+ Often scheduled meetings are continued in the organisation because 'it's Monday morning', even though their purpose has seized to exist.

+ Needing approval of a document by 4 different people to make sure that nothing can go wrong.

+ Filling out paperwork while the requested information is already available in another system.

+ Spending 4 weeks to create a perfect sales plan for the next year when you know the plan will be outdated within a month.

+ Add some examples of your own: ….

The world does not stand still or slow down- new competitors appear, clients demand ever more, and technology improves continuously-as a result, the ladder becomes a bottleneck. People start complaining about the ladder being obsolete, yet no one really does anything about it because the ladder has become part of the culture and the daily routine.

As time passes and co-workers change it often occurs that nobody in the organisation even remembers why certain ladders were built or why we continue to climb them. We just do, because 'it has always been like this'.

BRADY PYLE

HR EXECUTIVE @ NASA, HUSBAND, DAD TO 3, LEADERSHIP STUDENT, PRACTITIONER, SPEAKER, AND BLOGGER AT OUTOFTHISWORLDLEADERSHIP.COM

LOOKING IN THE MIRROR

Leadership starts with leading yourself, so your most powerful leadership tool is a mirror. You should know your strengths and weaknesses and be aware of your values all the time. Knowing who you are will help you to select the right people around you to have a good balance and be the best team. The mirror is also a great tool to use when you run into a conflict or when expectations aren't met. Instead of blaming others, start by looking in the mirror at your own actions. How did you contribute to the situation? Were your expectations clear? What could you have done differently to prevent the conflict? Pull out the mirror to be a more effective leader.

CELEBRATE FAILURES

At NASA, we are known as a "Failure is Not an Option" organization. While that served us well in rescuing the crew of Apollo 13, that culture permeated and inhibited innovation. To build a culture of innovation, we initiated a recognition program to celebrate failures. During the development of a new lunar lander, we lost a test vehicle.

NASA's Administrator pointed out that "Failure is part of the price of learning" and recognized the team with a "Lean Forward, Fail Smart" award. The team also widely shared lessons learned from this important development effort, helping build a culture that embraces appropriate risk-taking and the use of test failures to ultimately succeed.

Pictures © NASA

HOUSTON WE HAVE A PROBLEM

Most people will still remember the scene from Apollo 13 where the crew of astronauts and ground-control had to be very creative to solve a big technical failure. At that moment, they had to get rid of the standard procedures to face this crisis.

The solution was derived from a series of inductions, deductions, calculations, simulations, decisions, trials, errors, planning, re-planning, and execution, all driven by on-the-spot creativity, fuzzy logic, and incomplete data. Looking from a different perspective was essential to find a solution. And know, these are the same factors that drive many of our day-to-day innovations--innovations that surface, under pressure, in coping with crisis.

Check out the short videoclip to see this particular scene.

thechangemindset.video/houstonproblem

LEADING FRONT LINE ENGINEERS FOR 9 MONTHS

I had been Deputy HR Director in Houston for 3 years when I read "The Chief HR Officer" and learned that 75% of HR leaders in industry worked outside the HR function. While I had experience outside of NASA, I always worked in different HR functions. So, I took an opportunity to work for several months as a front-line leader of engineers - to get a different perspective about our technical culture and employee engagement. It was a great learning experience.

At the executive level, we have lot of discussions around change. We have very clear reasons why we want to go in a certain direction, but it was almost unbelievable how little information about the 'why' reached the frontline. This explained some resistance because people didn't know why they had to use a new system or follow a different approach. Since I returned to my senior HR position, I spent quite some time with my HR team to translate our plans and actions to all levels of the organization, which increased buy-in to changes we initiated and improved overall engagement levels.

HOW WOULD ... SOLVE THE BANANA PEEL PROBLEM?

* **The Health & Safety Manager** puts a big fence around the banana peel and makes sure that everybody who walks within 20 meters of it wears a helmet. They might even organise an awareness meeting to explain the dangers of a banana peel lying on the floor.

* **The HR Manager** checks if there is someone in the company who has banana peel pick-up-skills in their profile. If not, they will send a high-potential candidate on a 3 week long banana-peel-pick-up training to make sure that person has the right skills to do the task.

* **The Legal Counsellor** waits until somebody falls over the banana peel and then sues every banana producing company in the world.

* **The Innovation Manager** organises a brainstorm session with a multidisciplinary team to generate hundreds of ideas to solve this challenge. He then gathers the solutions on a one pager and delivers it to the CEO.

* **The Government Employee** hires a team of management consultants that come in, analyse the situation and deliver an extensive report explaining that there is a banana peel on the floor. They advise waiting for 4 weeks until the banana peel has rotted away.

* **The Quality Control Assessor** creates a checklist with relevant criteria (size, thickness, color, shape, ...), and does a risk-assessment of all possible scenarios depending on who may slip on the banana-peel.

* **The Agile Scrum Master** creates a Scrum Board, breaks up the epic "banana peel problem" into 15 Stories and 8 Tasks. He plans 4 sprints of 2 weeks for the estimated Work. Each morning the Scrum Master does a short stand-up meeting with the banana peel-developers and the banana peel product owner to assess whether the situation of the banana peel has changed.

* **The Company Coach** asks the banana peel if it hurts to lie on the floor. He then proceeds to reflect together on some options on how the banana peel could solve it is own problem.

* **The Visual Facilitator** takes a flipchart, draws the banana peel and listens carefully to all reactions from bystanders. Then he draws them, notes comments down, groups them. He then makes people voice what they now think the best course of action is.

* **The Junior Management Trainee** follows the 'problem'-procedure which means that they must print 7 documents from the internet where they fill out the problem and the possible consequences. He gets extra points if he can add a business plan with the necessary figures on how this will affect the quarterly results of the company. This document has to be signed by his direct boss who will discuss it in the next management meeting where they will take the 'right' decision. If he is lucky, he will be informed two months later about the decision.

* **The Communication Specialist** starts to collect quotes from leaders saying how critical removing the banana peel is in the company strategy. He then launches a communication campaign with videos, infographics and a roadshow to warn the employees about the dangers of a banana peel. A few months later, the team invites leaders to give an update on the status of the banana peel... but no one shows up. The management team has been so busy re-defining their strategy and re-aligning their organisation charts, that no one remembers where the cursed banana peel is or who (if anyone) was held accountable for removing it.

* **The Handyman or Cleaning Lady** sighs before picking up the banana peel, and throwing it in the nearest waste bin.

7 SOLID REASONS TO BUILD LADDERS

There are many reasons why ladders come into existence. After examining more than 500 'ladder' examples, we have defined 7 categories detailing how 'ladders are born'.

1. LACK OF CONNECTION WITH REALITY

The organisation is still living in the old world where things changed slowly. The world out there has moved on, but organisations are still stuck with outdated rules and procedures. Often, an entire industry is still applying outdated methods when that same industry is already being shook up by a new startup that has adapted the service or product to changed circumstances.

A perfect example of an industry that is lagging behind is the law practice. It is still very common to send faxes, print documents quadruple and jurisprudence itself is by default always running behind on society's reality. Recently a Dutch lawmaker wanted to speed up the judicial process and decided to accept a digital response for a certain procedure. This meant that instead of sending 4 copies of the same document the lawyer could send an email with the correct document. However - this is where genius strikes - the document in question had to be attached fourfold to make sure that the rule of quadruple was still applied.

Because of potential legal consequences, we still have to print out an entire contract, sign it page by page and then scan it back with the signature. There are perfectly operational digital services that could be used omitting the print to paper and back process, but those are not legally accepted yet.

On the subject of using faxes: loads of companies and people still mention a fax number on their business cards. If you ask around at the office, hardly anyone seems to know where a possible fax would arrive or if anyone would ever pick up on it. Do you still have a fax number on your business card?

2. UNDERESTIMATING THE COST OF CONTROL

In our attempt to try and control the world and reduce the risks, we often forget the cost of control. It also costs money, time and energy to keep the right procedures in place. However, we have a tendency to underrate these costs, only focusing on the things that can go wrong.

* An employee of a local government told me that it took her 45 minutes of work to ask to be reimbursed for a bus ticket she needed to go to a meeting in town. She had to log on to the internet, find the right document, fill out the document, ask for a signature from her finance department, scan the document and upload it in the right category. This excludes the time it took for the person at finance to process the request.

3. LACK OF TRUST

We don't trust other people. We have a tendency to try control everything - even if the result is the only thing that should be measured. Then we also attempt to control the process of how somebody achieves certain results. If we could completely trust someone, then we wouldn't need a system to control their behavior. This is without even knowing how it's going to happen.

* In most supermarkets, the self-checkout systems have become normal. Instead of having to go to a cashier, the customer scans the articles that they want and pays without interacting with a cashier. The idea is built on trust. (Most) customers actually pay for all the products that they have bought. Several studies showed that the cost of shoplifting (where the customer isn't trustworthy and doesn't scan all the articles) is outweighed by that of hiring a cashier, or longer waiting lines. The practice of shoplifting itself is easily discouraged by occasional random purchase ticket controls.

* If I want to purchase a new stapler at the office, I must download a purchase document, fill out the document and explain why I need this product. My manager then signs to approve the purchase. I then send the document to the administration who will log the document and connect it with a purchase order number. Following this the document is sent to the finance department who will sign it. The document goes back to administration to log the signatures and I will get the document back with the PO number, and only then can I order the stapler from the retailer.

WE APPLY THE SAME RULE TO EVERYONE

An obscure element that adds a lot to the proliferation of ladders and bureaucracy is the fact that we tend to instantly apply the same rule to everyone. Sometimes a certain procedure or rule is emphasised and applied temporarily to a small group of people. However, when applied to an entire organisation, it becomes less efficient.

* A Ministry wanted to stimulate more creative thinking within the organisation. They developed a digital management tool whereby employees could suggest ideas to improve their work. They had noticed that some of the ideas were quite vague and not really helpful. To upgrade the quality of the proposals, they assigned several idea-coaches to the workforce who helped formulate a more concrete idea. The idea-coach would sit down with the employee and after 15 minutes the quality of the idea would have increased significantly. With the best intentions, they decided that every person who came up with a new idea would have a meeting with the idea-coach to improve the quality. The result: less and less ideas were suggested because most employees didn't want to spend an extra 15 minutes with an idea-coach.

* In the Emergency Services Department of a hospital in the Netherlands, the staff can only create a new patient file if the patient has completed a range of screenings (suicide-intention, self-sustainability, mistreatment, malnutrition, …). This is relevant to a small percentage of patients but not for the majority (80%) of the cases - like a sprained ankle.

A SYSTEM IS ALWAYS A DELAYED VERSION OF REALITY

We will change a system because the old way is no longer effective. However, building a new system or procedure requires a lot of time: analysing the situation, planning, designing, prototyping, testing, training, support and creating backup systems before the new system is implemented. By the time people are used to the new system, it is very likely already outdated.

* A financial team needs 5 months at the end of their fiscal year to predict their annual budget for the next year. It costs a lot of time, energy and money (and even more meetings with all departments) to create this budget. In reality, the 'perfect' financial plan has to be superseded by an updated version - a few weeks after the final version is ready, due to the fast-changing market. Why do we spend so much time on planning, knowing that the reality will most likely be changed by the time we're done?

Another fact is that most people in the organisation use the yearly budget plan as a kind of guiding tool during the year. At the end of the financial year, they use it to point fingers at each other when mistakes or miscalculations need to be accounted for.

THE PROCEDURE BECOMES THE GOAL, LEADING TO COMPLEXITY

When procedures and systems are around for a long time, we sometimes forget the reason why the procedure was created in the first place. This often happens when the procedures have led to a complex layout like cross-department systems. They may even require a control system to make sure that all the rules are followed. In those cases, following the right procedure is more valued than looking at the added value the procedure provides. In extreme cases, this can even lead to situations where the procedures have an opposite effect to the original intention.

* Most government subsidy policies are intended to support the weaker/smaller/vulnerable parties in a certain industry. The procedures to apply for a subsidy have, over time, become so complex that the subsidies usually go to the organisations that have become experts in applying for subsidies. Sadly, most of the time these companies aren't the most deserving of financial aid

RISK AVERSION

We live in times where mistakes are hardly allowed. This differs from culture to culture. In the US, it is somewhat accepted to make a mistake and learn from it. In Europe, a few small mistakes are permissible, but in Asia people have an innate fear of doing something wrong or different.

In general, we are afraid to make mistakes. That is why we develop rules, procedures and systems to reduce the chance that mistakes will happen. We reduce the level of risk, but it can lead to a paradox where we have so many procedures and rules that people start to make more mistakes due to the complexity. In Belgium, it is even a specialisation in law practice to go for a mistrial or even an acquittal on procedural grounds.

* To promote a blog about my book on a business platform run by a big Belgian bank, I had agreed to give away ten books to the first ten people who would send a tweet about that blog. I would pay for the books, the bank would send them to the winners to make sure that their privacy was respected. It sounded easy and simple, but then the legal department heard that the bank would be involved in a Twitter competition. "What would happen if a participant came up with a dispute?", they asked. They needed to come up with contest rules to make sure that nothing could go wrong. Suddenly, more and more questions arose (what if somebody didn't have Twitter and wanted to participate? what if ...?).

All kinds of scenarios surfaced, and it took a month to be cleared. I don't know how much time, energy and money was spent by the bank (whilst involving people from legal, creating a selection committee who had to work out a procedure with contest rules, ...) where initially costs were estimated at €25 for the stamps.

RIDICULOUS RULES

+ France- schools must follow an 80-page document stipulating that children in day care centres can eat a quarter of a hard-boiled egg per meal, in nurseries half an egg and in primary or secondary schools one and a half eggs. Also in France, a French baguette is not allowed to be longer than 50-55 cm.

+ Victoria, Australia- only a licensed electrician is allowed to change a light bulb.

+ Alabama, America- it is illegal to be blindfolded while driving a vehicle.

+ England- it is an act of treason to place a postage stamp bearing the British monarch upside down.

+ Miami, Florida- it is illegal to skateboard in a police station. Also in Florida, unmarried women who parachute on Sundays can be jailed.

+ Quitnan, Georgia- chickens are not allowed to cross the road

+ In Paulding, Ohio- policemen are allowed to bite a dog if they think it will calm the dog down

+ Rhode Island- You may not sell toothpaste and a toothbrush to the same customer on a Sunday

+ Wyoming- You may not take a picture of a rabbit between January and April without an official permit

+ Washington- A motorist with criminal intentions must stop at the city limits and telephone the chief of police before he enters the town

+ Hong Kong- a law allows a wife to kill her husband if she finds him cheating. However, she must kill him with her bare hands.

+ In Singapore, selling chewing gum is illegal and can lead to a prison sentence of up to two years.

I'm not sure whether all of these laws still apply today, but these rules and laws sometimes oblige public forces and private businesses to go to absurd and costly lengths to obey them. The key principle is to bring back common sense to save an enormous amount of money (and frustrations).

A lot of Ladders are Created by Ourselves

Government and corporate hierarchies are mostly blamed for this red tape and bureaucracy, but a fair amount of all these ladders are created by ourselves. Research done by Deloitte discovered in late 2014 that the majority of individual managers spend up to eight hours per week complying with self-imposed red tape. Many of us are held back by ropes we tied around our own necks.

Deloitte also looked at the problem of bureaucracy in their own business and that led to running regular surveys asking employees questions like 'What is stopping you from doing your job?' and 'What are the dumb things we do?'

IKEA offers a beautiful example of fighting against senseless internal regulations. Once a year all IKEA managers have to work on the shop floor for a week. They call this the 'anti-bureaucracy week.' The initiative is designed to give managers a deep, personal understanding of IKEA's customers. It allows for an ideal opportunity for management to truly understand the issues employees are facing daily. Once the leaders of the organisation have experienced the side-effects of certain procedures and decisions they created, it is a lot easier to get rid of some of those ladders.

3 GRAMS OF COMMON SENSE

From time to time people call me the "Creativity Guy", and that pleases me (obviously). Although I find that the title does not really reflect my core message. I love that I can stimulate creativity, but if you ask me, I would rather be known as the "Common Sense" guy because in 95% of the cases I believe common sense will take you further than sheer creativity. I'm a strong believer of the idiom 'if it isn't broken, don't fix it'. Why should you change something if you are happy with the results of the old process or system? Only look for alternatives when you're no longer happy with the old route. It could be that the quality of the process no longer satisfies you, or you want to explore a new market, you need to find new talent in a very competitive market, and so on. It doesn't make sense to try and reinvent the wheel constantly.

If you're asking questions about every single process that you've installed, or you want to invent a new process for every task you're doing, it would probably lead to chaos. If you have no guidelines or directions to evaluate which processes are worth investigating, you would just keep yourself occupied but it would not necessarily lead to more efficiency or quick innovation.

In our western society, we have built a myriad of systems and procedures. This means we are busier checking boxes and following all kind of procedures, without knowing the reasons why. In some environments, it seems that using common sense has become subservient to the checklists with rules.

We have created a society of 'sheeple'. We gladly follow rules without wondering why we have this rule in the first place. We don't need or want to see the connection between a certain procedure and the result. Sometimes (and this happens often in large companies), the procedures even lead to an outcome opposite to the goal we were aiming at. The same goes for the ladders in our heads; we are guided by a lot of (conscious & unconscious) judgement all the time.

COMPUTER SAYS NO

is the popular name given to an attitude in customer service in which the default response is to check with information stored or generated electronically. Decisions are made based on that, apparently without using common sense- showing a level of un-helpfulness whereby more could be done to reach a mutually satisfactory outcome, but is not. The name gained popularity through the British sketch comedy 'Little Britain'.

thechangemindset.video/ computersaysno

The Project Management Bible

Before the merging of two big mobile operators, one of them had a very elaborate project management system. There were 45 templates (yep, 45) that needed to be filled out and project managers typically spent about one third of their time filling out the paper-work. There were 5 people employed full time to monitor the paperwork. In 2008, there was even a one-year program set up to find and fix the gaps in the control system. This led to a "Project Manager Bible" that consisted of 400 pages. The team that updated the Bible was very proud and their belief was: "We are the best in the industry". Procedure upon procedure upon ... During the merger, the new organisation said: "No way we're going to adopt this. The level of complexity is too high." Common sense, agility, trust and empowerment were adopted as important concepts to work with. The number and scope of templates were drastically reduced and only the necessary ones were kept. Guidelines were drafted as a reference point. This led to 80% less overhead costs.

The Team Meeting Turned into Metrics

"With our senior leadership we went 6 levels down in the organisation to experience first-hand how our well-intended plans were put into practice. A few months earlier, we had implemented pre-shift meetings; i.e. a quick meeting between colleagues before starting their work. The senior leaders wanted to create camaraderie and a feeling of belonging and care. As it turned out, cascading the suggestion down 5 or 6 levels, it had evolved into a monstrous documentation exercise.

The reason being that during the translation process onto the floor, it had become a metric on a scorecard. The 'system' requires that all metrics on a scorecard have to be written down to prove it. Sadly, the system was not comfortable enough without official metrics. Thus, they had created a new (redundant) workflow where the initial idea of camaraderie and belonging was nowhere to be found. This shows that a well-intended new approach can have an adverse effect, which is mainly caused by a lack of a clear common understanding of why we do what we do at all times".

REZA MOUSSAVIAN

SENIOR VICE PRESIDENT HR DIGITAL AND INNOVATION @ DEUTSCHE TELEKOM, KEYNOTE SPEAKER, DIGITAL DISRUPTION, FUTURE OF WORK, ENTHUSIASM, DIGITAL WORKSPACE, SALSA DJ

MY THREE TIPS FOR LEADERS WHO WANT TO CREATE AN AGILE ENVIRONMENT FOR THEIR EMPLOYEES

1. Just start with new initiatives (on a small scale) instead of organising meetings & writing reports what can be done. Get into action & learn quickly.

2. Dare to kill your darlings. The world is changing fast and we need to make resources (time, energy, money) free for the products & services of the future.

3. Ask yourself the question: do you really believe in an agile organisation (are you willing to re-think certain processes radically) or do you just do it as a kind of marketing trick? If a CEO shows up wearing some sneakers doesn't mean that he's willing to re-think his whole organisation radically.

ORGANISING NIGHT OF TRUTH EVENTS

We have already organised Night of Truth events in our "Leadership Academy" where the participants come on stage and share some failures and the connected learnings. And it was a huge success because since then, other departments started to organise their own Night of Truth events and the attendance is really good. These nights are part of a broader vision to create a more innovative culture.

WE NEED MOVEMENT

Just start with new initiatives (on a small scale) instead of organising meetings & writing reports what can be done? Get into action & learn quickly. Most HR departments or professionals make the mistake of coming up with new policies and rules to make sure that change is applied in the organisation. I don't work like that. I want to show relevant business cases. I rather work with a small team and have a tangible, concrete outcome instead of coming up with 'theoretical' training for 1000 people which won't have that much impact.

(Business) People want to see results. We focus a lot of creating success stories because they provide some 'soft pressure' on the business to strive for change. We share the business story - what was the challenge, how did we help and what was the output & result of our intervention. We let other talk about us and provide us with recommendations because they trust their peers. It's that movement that we need and that's what people talk about.

CULTURE INNOVATION LABS

Most innovation labs are mainly focussed on developing new products and services. They are often placed far away from the company - in a figurative and literal way - to give them more freedom to experiment. But they shouldn't be that far from the 'big organisation' because that's the place where we need movement.

Can we have a Culture Innovation lab instead that focusses on challenging the status quo of the corporate paradigms. That lab should explore possibilities in the future, challenge the status quo and support the organisation in taking the first steps to a new future.

CYA, INSTRUCTION CREEP & OTHER BUREAUCRATIC DISEASES

Cover your ass or C.Y.A. describes an activity, usually in a work-related or bureaucratic context, done by an individual to protect him or herself from possible subsequent criticism or legal penalties.

Instruction creep occurs when instructions increase in number and size over time until they are unmanageable. It can be insidious and damaging to the success of large groups such as corporations, originating from ignorance of the KISS principle and resulting in overly complex (as opposed to simplified) procedures that are often misunderstood, followed with great irritation or ignored.

Busywork - In business and work settings, people may engage in busy work simply to appear like they are busy and productive. The primary goal of maintaining an appearance of activity is to protect their employment status.

Red tape is an idiom that refers to excessive regulation or rigid conformity to formal rules that are considered redundant or bureaucratic, and hinders or prevents action or decision-making. It is usually applied to governments, corporations, and other large organizations.

Data-Obesitas - obsession to collect as much data as possible without really knowing why and how to use that data.

BOHICA - Bend over, here it comes again. This term is commonly used in the workplace when a new change project has been announced. It refers to the fact that a lot of the change projects fail, and it forces everybody to readapt to the new plans of the next boss once again.

'Corporate Myopia' - a short-sighted and inward-looking approach to marketing that focuses on the needs of the company instead of defining the company and its products in terms of the customer's needs and wants.

Administrivia: routine paperwork and other administrative tasks that are regarded as trivial, uninteresting, and time-consuming

"BUREAUCRACY IS THE ART OF MAKING THE POSSIBLE IMPOSSIBLE."

JAVIER PASCUAL SALCEDO

The System Can't Hear You

I absolutely believe that systems and procedures have a lot of value and most of the growth and welfare in society comes from these procedures that make us more efficient and effective. That being said, in our search for increasing efficiency, boundaries have been crossed. We have created very complex, rigid systems where we allow people to use the system as an excuse to deliver mediocre results, sometimes even results opposite to the real goals of the company.

Seth Godin argues that the system can't hear you. Only people can. People are seduced to believe that they don't have power over the system. It is easier to say that they are just a cog in the machine that is a lot bigger than themselves. In fact, it's not the systems who misrepresent us, waste resources like time, money and energy, support an unfair status quo or screw things up. It is the people who use the system who are responsible for these things. If we cared enough, we could make it change. Before that can happen, you need to switch your mindset from being a 'victim' who can't help it, to being a 'potentialist' who's ready to explore an alternative route, with the guts to experiment.

REAL LADDER STORIES

When I deliver my presentation around 'the change mindset', I start my story with an actual ladder and banana on stage to explain the metaphor. I put the ladder's legs on top of the banana peel and climb over it to demonstrate the absurdity of the situation. When I deliver my presentations nearby, I normally bring my own ladder with me but when I need to take a flight, I have to request a ladder from the organiser of the event.

Getting this done, having this physical ladder on stage (the banana is usually not a problem), has already led to the emergence of several other metaphorical ladders.

QUALITY CERTIFICATE FOR A LADDER

When I checked if it was okay to bring my own ladder to their workplace, I was requested to bring the ladder a day in advance. The reason being that all materials at the plant needed to be checked in order to receive a quality certificate. Luckily the event-organiser found an elephant path past security to avoid this procedure.

CLIMBING A LADDER IS FORBIDDEN

I had requested a ladder from the events company a few weeks in advance thinking it a minor issue. The day before the speech I checked to see if they had managed to find a ladder. When the event organisers and the hotel manager heard that I was going to climb the ladder on stage, issues arose around Australia's strict health and safety laws. At one point, a total of 5 people (3 from the events company & 2 from the hotel) were involved in the ladder discussion. It ended with a compromise: I could have a ladder on stage, but I couldn't climb it. The general manager of the events company even had to sign a waiver to confirm this.

When I first received this news, I was disappointed that I couldn't perform my 'ladder' show. However, after 2 minutes I realised that this was probably one of the best things that could have happened. It's the perfect example of the metaphorical ladders you might need to climb before getting a physical ladder.

BUY YOUR OWN LADDER

When the legal, health & safety departments heard that I needed a ladder to climb up, they came up with a very creative solution. They advised me to buy my own ladder and arrange for it's delivery to the venue (I could reclaim the costs). This way they, as a company, wouldn't be liable for any risks. Brilliant.

SHOW ME YOUR TRAVEL INSURANCE

Before I could start my speaking tour in Australia, the organisers asked me to send a copy of my travel and professional insurance. This was to ensure that if something went wrong while climbing the ladder, they wouldn't be liable. I met trouble when I discovered I had to switch the Flemish contract to an English version - it was an arduous process (I even had to switch insurance companies to get this done).

Picture © Konstantin Gastmann

BRING YOUR OWN LADDER

The advice that I now give to most event organisers (especially for smaller events) is to bring their own ladder from home. Avoid mentioning this to other departments in the company (certainly not legal or health & safety). This works quite well. I also liked the approach of one manager in a large energy company: he called the technical facilities department just before my presentation would start. He said he quickly needed a ladder to replace a lamp. The guy brought the ladder to the hallway and the manager promised to return it within an hour.

THE BANANA CHALLENGE

The ladder is in most cases the most challenging element to arrange but in one case, getting a banana turned out to be quite an ordeal. That day my presentation was in the early morning (before the shops opened) and I forgot to bring my banana. The night before I had dinner in a restaurant/hotel and hoped that they would have a banana for me. I asked the waiter if they had a banana and yes, he confirmed they did.

Unfortunately, he didn't know if he was allowed to give me a banana. He had to check with the manager and two minutes later, the manager was at our table announcing that they could not give me a 'raw' banana. Food inspection regulations prohibits them from serving their guests raw food. I even tried to order a banana-split from the dessert menu (without the ice and chocolate, but with the skin), but my attempts were futile. The following morning, I did manage to find an apple, so my presentation became "Ladders & Apples".

"DON'T MIND THE CHANGE.

CHANGE YOUR MIND."

CYRIEL KORTLEVEN

ROB LILWALL

GLOBAL KEYNOTE SPEAKER, NATIONAL GEOGRAPHIC ADVENTURER, AUTHOR, CHANGE, GROWTH MINDSET, RESILIENCE, BORN IN BRITAIN, LIVING IN HONG KONG, LOVING HUSBAND AND FATHER. TORTURED SOUL!

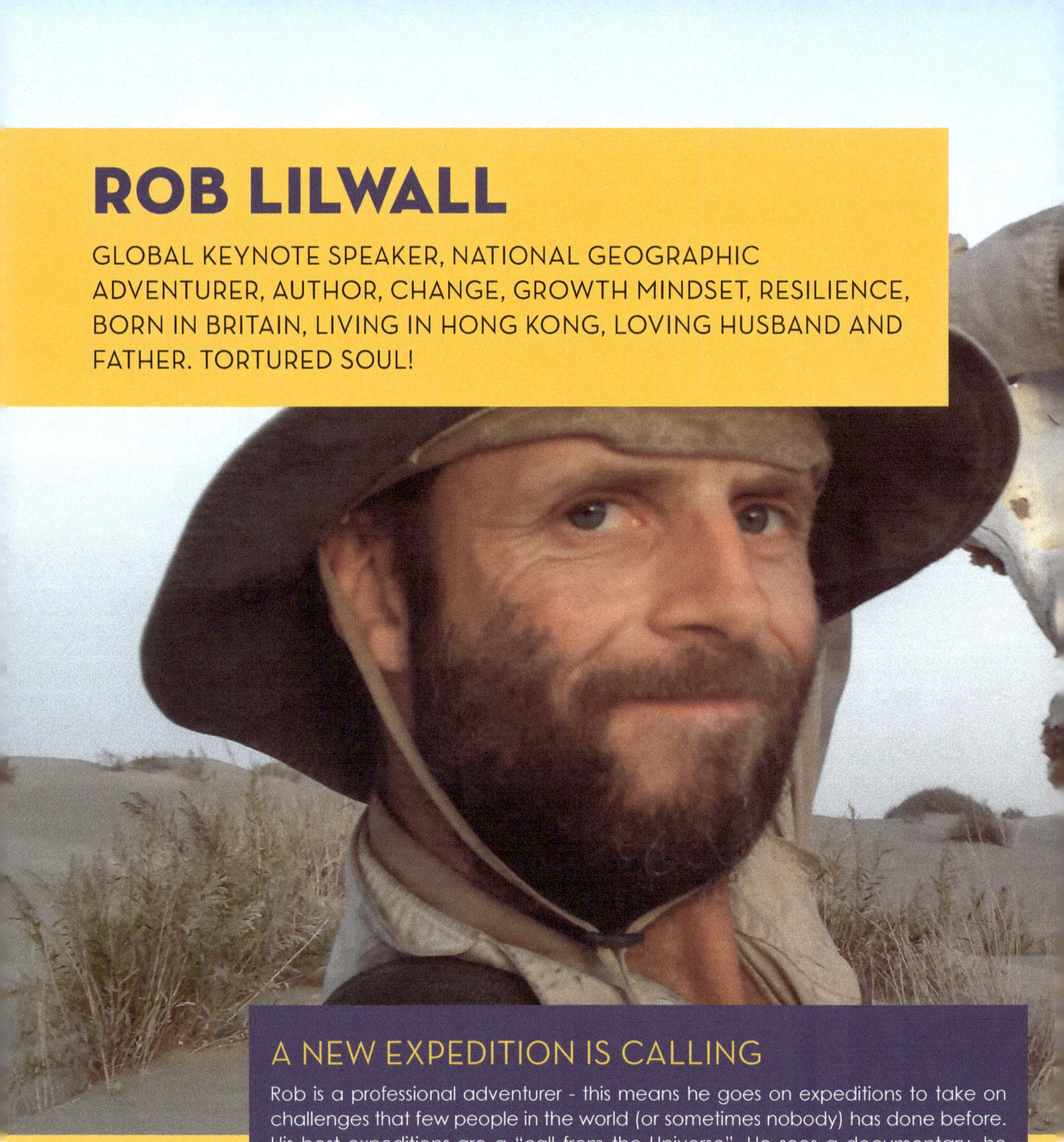

Image Credits: Rob Lilwall

A NEW EXPEDITION IS CALLING

Rob is a professional adventurer - this means he goes on expeditions to take on challenges that few people in the world (or sometimes nobody) has done before. His best expeditions are a "call from the Universe". He sees a documentary, he hears a radio program, or just looks at a map ... and then something bizarre happens. An idea is planted that can grow into a bigger idea ... a plan ... a commitment ... a research mission ... an expedition. Those expeditions are the real and authentic ones. The same is true for any professional. They come to you ... you just have to be aware of the 'Call'.

Danger arises if you let your rationale decide on which expedition to do next, because your mind is already occupied with thoughts on how you can use certain parts for a new presentation or book. Consequently, the quality and authenticity of that expedition will suffer. And you will enjoy it less.

DOING A LOT OF EXPERIMENTS

Planning is crucial when going on an expedition - it's a matter of life or death. It's quite easy to plan an adventure on paper, but you have to do a lot of experiments (or small actions) to see if things will be successful or not. One example is my walk from Mongolia to Hong Kong - a trip of 6 months where I had to carry my heavy rucksack. In my training, I would go on a 3 hour walk with 75% of the weight, assuming I could do the same thing on the actual trip. But walking for 12 hours a day for 6 months, on the actual expedition, was completely different. I really underestimated the pain and I should have tried the real thing instead of spending time planning.

For my latest expedition – a 71 day solo attempt across China's Taklamakan Desert, I did a lot more experiments. I was going to cross the desert with a home-made beach cart. This time, I did many experiments at our local beach. To simulate the weight that I would be carrying in the desert, I asked some local kids to jump on my cart to better understand the strength I needed to pull the cart. During a longer experiment in the desert itself, I found out that fixing the tires would be a real challenge in certain areas of the desert. My advice is, don't spend all your time on making great plans, which are often based on assumptions. Rather try to 'simulate the real situation' as fast as possible because then you can immediately adjust your 'big' plan.

THE FLOATING RUCKSACK

Because most adventures are one big 'innovation' process since nobody has tried it before, you need to think out the box.. Of course, you can learn from people who have done something similar. But in most cases, you have to come up with new solutions both in the planning and on the expedition itself. Expect that the unexpected..

For example, on my last adventure, I had to cross a big river. I knew that the river was there, but I didn't know how deep it would be, and I was carrying a 30kg rucksack. What happens is that your brain starts to think in an unconscious way about solutions. In this case, I knew that I fogotten some empty water bottles at my previous camp-site. Suddenly it occurred to me that I should go back and get those bottles to put them in my rucksack as floating materials to help cross the river. It worked - except for the fact that I had to swim across the river 12 times because the weight in my rucksack was too heavy to go only once.

A CHANGI

Do you choose a fixed or growth mindset?

Making (conscious) choices is not an easy task, but it is possible. If you make a conscious choice to develop your potential, beautiful things can be achieved. If you do not dare to make bold choices, then life will probably deal you a mediocre hand. What do you choose?

G MINDSET

A FIXED OR GROWTH MINDSET

A mindset is a belief that orients the way we handle situations; the way we sort out what is going on and what we should do. Our mindsets help us to spot opportunities, but they can trap us in self-defeating cycles.

Carol Dweck is one of the world's leading researchers in the field of motivation. In her book 'Mindset' she explains that our mindset is responsible for our self-awareness, self-esteem, creativity, ability to face challenges and our resilience to setbacks. Our mindset is the view that you have of your qualities and characteristics; where they come from, and whether they can change.

There are two extreme ends on either side of the spectrum:

+ A fixed mindset comes from the belief that you have qualities that you can no longer change. You are who you are. Characteristics such as intelligence, personality and creativity are fixed traits which can't be developed.

+ A growth mindset comes from the belief that your basic qualities are things you can cultivate through effort. Everybody can change and grow through practice and experience, knowing that human beings differ greatly in their talents, interests or temperaments.

You can of course find yourself somewhere in the middle of that spectrum or you can lean a certain way in one area of your life and a different way in other areas.

Your mindset influences a lot of things in life. For example, if you have a more fixed mindset when it comes to creativity, you believe that you can reach a certain level of creativity, but no more. Maybe you believe that you're not a creative person at all.

You don't believe that extra effort or learning will bring you to a higher level, and this is reflected in your behaviour. If someone asks you for new ideas, you don't devote a lot of effort to come up with any because you believe they won't be good anyway. You avoid brainstorm sessions because they're just mumbo jumbo and you won't add any added value. In fact, what you are doing is depriving yourself from new creativity methods and the experience of generating new ideas. This results, of course, in the confirmation that you're not a very creative person, compared to others who you assume are better at generating fresh ideas.

Your whole personality can be influenced by your mindset. If you have a fixed 'negative' mindset about yourself (which can of course be caused by past experiences), then it's quite hard to break through these fixed thinking patterns. Because your brain is looking for situations that will re-enforce its belief system. You block opportunities even before they have started- (that new colleague won't like me, so I'll try to avoid her. Your strange behaviour may cause her to feel and look visibly uncomfortable, which you again interpret as confirmation that she doesn't like you). It's a spiral of negative thinking where the fixed mindset stands in the way of development and change.

A growth mindset is a starting point for change. But people still need to decide for themselves where their efforts toward change would be most valuable.

You can choose to change your mindset! It will of course take time and effort, but you have that choice at this moment.

The first step is being aware of your own mindset. How do you look at the world? Are you committed to embracing a different mindset? Do you want to change your own reality?

Mindsets are beliefs; beliefs about your-self and your most basic qualities. Think about your intelligence, your talents, your personality. Are these qualities simply fixed traits, carved in stone, end of story? Or are they things you can cultivate through-out your life?

People with a fixed mindset believe that their traits are just givens. They have a certain amount of intelligence and talent and noth-ing can change that. If they have this in abun-dance, they're all set but if they don't... People in this mindset worry about their traits and how adequate they are. They feel they have something to prove to themselves and others.

On the other hand, people with a growth mindset see their qualities as things that can be developed through dedication and effort. Sure, they're happy if they're brainy or talented, but that's just the starting point. They understand that no one has ever accomplished great things - not Mozart, Darwin, or Michael Jordan - without years of passionate practice and learning.

Mindset
by Carol Dweck

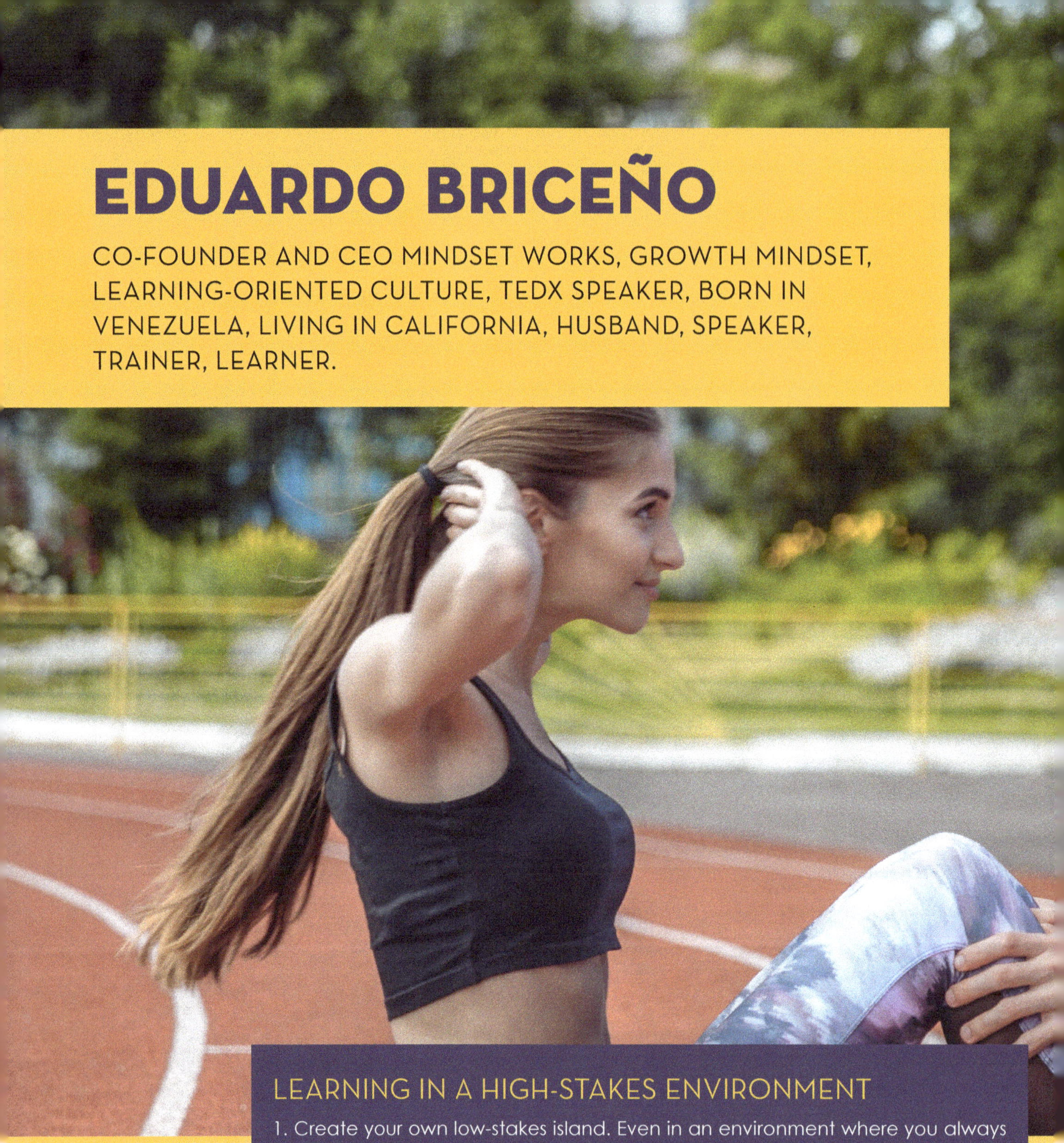

EDUARDO BRICEÑO

CO-FOUNDER AND CEO MINDSET WORKS, GROWTH MINDSET, LEARNING-ORIENTED CULTURE, TEDX SPEAKER, BORN IN VENEZUELA, LIVING IN CALIFORNIA, HUSBAND, SPEAKER, TRAINER, LEARNER.

LEARNING IN A HIGH-STAKES ENVIRONMENT

1. Create your own low-stakes island. Even in an environment where you always have to be in performance mode, you can start with defining some domains in which you want to improve. Then you can improve in small ways. You could find a mentor or a colleague to share some learnings, or plan some time for learning activities like reading some books or watching a TED talk.

2. Keep executing and observe, reflect and adjust your behaviour afterwards. How did a certain meeting with a high-stake client go? What went well? What could be improved? What are the next steps needed to grow?

3. Become a role model in the high-stakes environment. Start with sharing your learnings and mistakes; create a safe zone where your colleagues can do the same, and give feedback to each other.

A LEARNING AND PERFORMANCE ZONE

The 'performance zone' is that moment when you're doing something as best as you can. You're executing. If you are a tennis player, then you're in the performance zone when you're playing a game. You want to win, so you apply all your techniques and strategies in the best way possible to win the game. But, if you're having trouble with your backhand topspin, you will avoid that move because you want to avoid mistakes and lost points.

The 'learning zone' is the moment when you focus on becoming better. You concentrate on the things that you haven't mastered yet (in this case, the backhand topspin). You will practice this move (with a coach) during training sessions to grow your tennis skills. At that moment, it's expected to make mistakes and observe them. You reflect on how you can adjust your technique to become better.

In most organisations, people try to be in the performance zone the entire time. Making mistakes is undesirable all of the time, and you're always in the execution phase. As a consequence, we're doing the best we can, but we're never getting better. We're stagnating. This can be very dangerous for an organisation (and an individual) because the world is changing, and continuous learning is becoming crucial. Successful organisations understand that their employees need time and opportunities to learn. There are many ways to support a learning environment, like clarifying how you want people to learn, having leaders role model learning visibly, and rewarding people who learn & share. It also helps to have a stimulating physical learning environment. once.

FOUR TYPES OF MISTAKES

Not every mistake is the same. Eduardo defines 4 different types of mistakes:

The Stretch Mistakes

'Stretch mistakes' happen when we're working to expand our current abilities. We're trying to do something that is beyond what we already can do without help, so we're bound to make some errors. When a mistake happens, reflect, identify what we can learn and adjust your approach to a more proactive stance, until you master the new level.

The 'Aha' Moment Mistakes

So, you do something as intended, but then realize that it was the wrong thing to do. There's a moment of surprise that makes you realize you need to do things in a different way. For example- you want to help a friend (assuming that help is always welcome), but we find out that the person didn't want help at that moment. Asking for feedback is a good way to learn from these mistakes.

The Sloppy Mistakes

These kinds of errors happen when you do something that you are already familiar with, in an incorrect way, due to lack of concentration. It's a signal to enhance our focus, attention or processes.

The High-Stakes Mistakes

You want to minimize these high-stakes mistakes because there's a lot to lose-sometimes it can be catastrophic or dangerous to make mistakes in these situations. You don't want to experiment with driving blindfolded, or setting out to try out new techniques during a sport championship. It's the moment to perform.

YOU ALWAYS

One of my own mantras for several years has been 'you always have a choice.' This creed was born almost 20 years ago when I first got into contact with creative thinking. Before that, I was thinking according to the paradigm of economics which stated that every question has one logical answer, no discussion. Unfortunately, as I discovered, the world isn't a logical or rational place.

Thanks to creative thinking, I could always discover alternative solutions. From a mathematical point of view, the answer to the question 1 + 1 has indeed one clear answer. But if you look at it from a more creative point of view, it could also be 11 putting the ones next to each other or it could become a plus-sign if you laid one horizontally on top of the other. There is not always one solution to a certain problem.

This new insight was quite a life-changing event for me. Suddenly it became clear that you always have a choice. You can always choose a different alternative if your current situation isn't working anymore.

However, I don't have a choice in everything.

I can't choose the weather and I can't choose whether my partner will be in a good mood or not. That is of course true. But I can choose how I respond to the weather or the mood of my partner. Even in extreme cases - for example, a thief tries to steal money from me - I can make a decision: my money or my life. Or, I could try and disarm the aggressor, or find a way to escape or .... I don't intend going any further on theoretical discussions in these extreme situations.

In 99,9% of the cases, we have a lot more freedom of choice about the way we are thinking, feeling and the way we behave than we think.

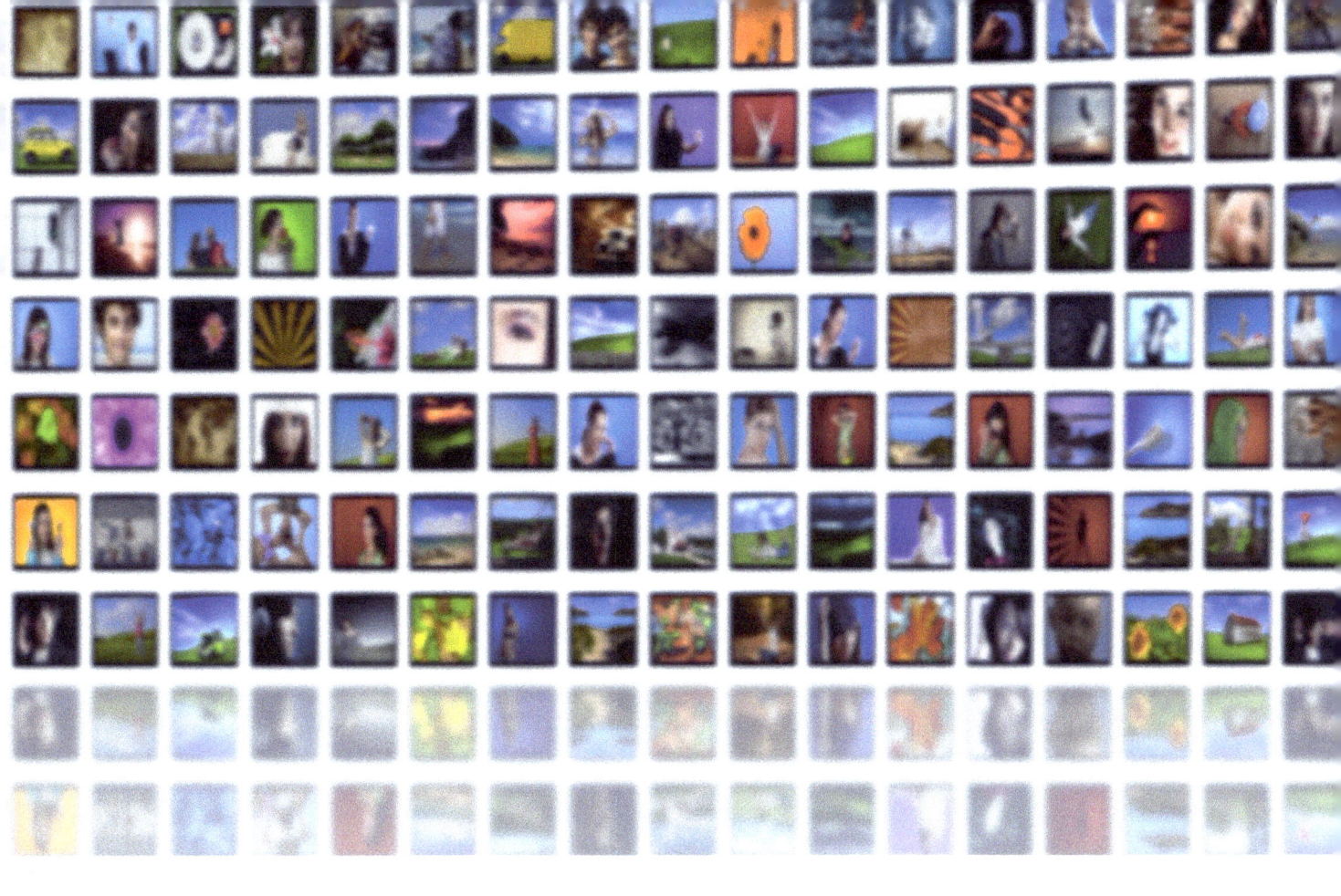

HAVE A CHOICE, RIGHT?

You rarely have a choice

If you always make conscious life decisions, then why are so many people still stuck in situations that they don't like? Why are so many people (myself included) not living up to all their dreams when they can choose to attempt it. Why do many people (unconsciously) not make those choices? That's where our biology kicks in. Only some of our thoughts, feelings and behaviours are preceded by conscious intentions. Most of the time, we operate on an autopilot with our unconscious mind at the steering wheel. Our conscious brains can only handle roughly 40 bits of information a second, while our unconscious minds can handle 11 million bits of information per second *.

Our unconscious brain is fast, instinctive and emotional. The conscious part of the brain is slower, more deliberate and logical. Our unconscious brain cares about 2 things: survival and maintaining the status quo (because the status quo preserves energy, which increases the chances of survival). The decisions that our unconscious brain is making are highly context-dependent. Whatever is going on at that moment - the weather, your state of mind, the time of the day, the last thing you ate or saw or felt - can influence your thoughts and decisions.

Does this mean that your unconscious brain is sabotaging the conscious brain? No. It is simply a different system. But how can I make a conscious choice (and change my life for the long-term)?

Does this mean that I have to accept that my unconscious mind is always the master of my thoughts? Must I stop making conscious choices to improve my life (and get out of situations where I'm not happy)? Absolutely not. However, don't assume for a second that it will be easy. The 'trick' is to use the substantial power of the unconscious brain. How? By creating a clear pattern. Our brain is wired to create habits and if we do something often enough (especially if it's tied to an external cue and reward), it will become a second nature. It's not will-power or self-control that we need to focus on; it's all about consistency and perseverance.

Repeat a certain habit that you want to achieve. Jocelyn Campbell describes a 4-step process in her article '7 Self-Help Myths that are Keeping You Stuck':

1. Create an intention (be specific, have a clear vision of the outcome, set a deadline).

E.g. I want to lose 5 kg and will complete a 20 km run in August this year.

2. Determine how you are going to keep your focus on the intention. What's the cue that could trigger a certain habit? This is an important step because it's the moment that puts things into motion.

E.g. I will place my running shoes next to the bed before I go to sleep.

3. Identify what you will do when things don't go according to plan. Be sure that things will go awry - it's not easy to predict what can happen, but you can probably already imagine 3 or 4 scenarios that will make it harder to persevere your new habit.

E.g. if it's rainy, my first task for the day is to go to the gym and run on the treadmill.

4. Reward yourself when you follow through.

Eg. I will get a nice breakfast after my run.

You can reprogram your automatic behaviour so it aligns better with the conscious intentions of your life. Oftentimes, reframing certain habits isn't sexy or exciting, but you have to stick to the process, be patient and persevere.

"LIFE IS A MATTER OF CHOICES, AND EVERY CHOICE YOU MAKE MAKES YOU."

JOHN C. MAXWELL

THE ART OF CHOOSING

Sheena Iyengar studies how we make choices -- and how we feel about the choices we make. At TEDGlobal, she talks about both trivial choices (Coke vs. Pepsi) and profound ones, sharing her groundbreaking research that has uncovered some surprising attitudes about our decisions.

thechangemindset.video/artofchoosing

thechangemindset.video/hardchoices

HOW TO MAKE HARD CHOICES?

Here's a talk that could literally change your life. Which career should I pursue? Should I break up- or get married?! Where should I live? Big decisions like these can be agonizingly difficult. That's because we think about them the wrong way, says philosopher Ruth Chang. She offers a powerful new framework for shaping who we truly are.

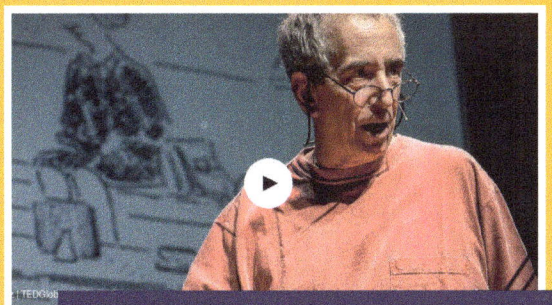

thechangemindset.video/paradox-choice

THE PARADOX OF CHOICE

Psychologist Barry Schwartz takes aim at a central tenet of western societies: freedom of choice. In Schwartz's estimation, choice has made us not freer, but more paralyzed; not happier but more dissatisfied..

7 WAYS TO LIVE A MEDIOCRE LIFE!

A lot of people are afraid of reaching their full potential. It's indeed a path where you have to dare to dream big, make difficult choices, commit, be persistent and accept failure in order to learn and continue. For those people who love the status quo, here are some tips to live a mediocre life.

1. Keep your dreams very realistic. Make sure that SMART actions are your mantra. Don't even think about doing something bigger than you can imagine. Don't even bother to imagine because that only leads to despair and disillusionment.

2. Listen to all the advice of others. Certainly, to the people who shout loudest and have never tried it themselves. It's absolutely true when they proclaim that 'it won't work anyway'. They are 100% correct in saying that if you never try to achieve your idea.

3. JDo normal - no crazy stuff. The world is already full of crazy people who want to do impossible things. Most of them won't achieve their goals anyway. Okay, a few of them will. But those are the exceptions. If you stay normal and behave within the 'normal' limits, you will be fine. Hopefully.

4. Be complacent. Do you know about the risks of a new idea? There are always risks - certainly in our perception. The status quo is not a bad place. Nothing changes. You do the same as the day before. No surprises. It can be a bit boring ... okay- very boring but hey, you can't have everything in life.

5. Laziness just has a bad name. It's not that bad to be lazy. Always choose the easiest way to achieve a goal. Don't take an extra step or put in some extra effort. It requires energy. Okay, you might miss out on some opportunities, but who said life is about 'having it all'?

6. Always look at the world from your point of view. Stay at home as much as possible because the world is a dangerous place. In a different country, they have a different culture and they behave very strangely. Don't go there because you might broaden your view and that might complicate your life. Having a small world view is easier.

7. Don't commit yourself. Perseverance is hard work - it costs time, money and energy to get somewhere. Spend a lot of time creating lots of disclaimers to make sure that they can never blame you for something. It's easier to stay where you are. Just hope that something extraordinary will happen, or maybe you get lucky.

You Can't Steer a Parked Car

An Australian colleague of mine, Michael McQueen, shared a great story in his book 'Momentum' about taking decisions to keep moving. He says that sometimes we get stuck in the trap of analysis paralysis - holding off on taking action because you want to consider all possible options. The danger is that you lose momentum and don't get to the action.

His dad told him 'You can't steer a parked car'. Don't wait for the perfect moment or until you have all the information, but get moving because you can always adjust the direction once you're on your way. And it's true ... you can't steer a parked car - it won't have any effect. However, when the car is moving, slowly or even in the wrong direction, it is possible to adjust course down the track.

ANOTHER 7 YEARS AND I CAN RETIRE

A few years ago, I had the chance to collaborate with 6 other colleagues during a week of creativity. A large governmental organisation had asked us to stimulate creativity in their local offices in Flanders (Belgium). We had permission to walk freely through their offices and visit the different departments. On those visits, we would catch the attention of a group of employees and give them a quick creativity boost. We had prepared several short exercises and practical tools to create awareness in the organisation for openness and creativity. We left beer coasters behind with tips to on maintaining a creative mindset.

A few people loved it and immediately wanted to apply some of the stuff in their daily jobs. Most people liked it. For others it was a fun break in between the normal activities. A few people couldn't care less, but the reaction of one guy really struck me. He was sitting in the back of the office. We had already done a few exercises with colleagues on his floor. I thought he must be quite busy, so I just wanted to give him a beer coaster. When he saw me approaching him, he jumped up and shouted "All this is nonsense. Nothing is going to change here anyway." And then he joyfully added "only another 7 years and then I can retire."

I was quite shocked that somebody could be so apathetic as to stay in a job that he apparently didn't like for a period of 7 years. I just gave him the beer coaster and wished him a nice day.

POTENTIALISM

'Potentialism' as a word popped up in my head during an interview with Nic Askew (soul- biographies). I had no clue if the word already existed or not. After some research, I found out that others have used the word potentialism before, but mostly in a more spiritual way. There's absolutely nothing wrong with that, but I prefer a more pragmatic and down-to-earth definition.

'Potentialism' is the process of exploring your capacity to grow as a person or professional.

It's about making and carrying out conscious decisions and actions to see how you can grow those latent talents you have. If you decide to strive to fulfill your potential, then I would call you a potentialist.

Take Full Responsibility for your Potential

Most people don't dare to take full responsibility for their own potential. It's a lot easier to hide behind rules, procedures, agreements, systems and blame others instead of exploring different paths to fulfill their dreams. We think that it's easier and safer to ignore our big dreams than to take full responsibility for them. It feels safer to stay in the current situation with a job that may not allow you to use all your skills, but at least you get paid. Safer to surround yourself with like-minded people who support your safe mode and confirm that the world is a dangerous place. It is equally safe to stay with your partner who doesn't love you unconditionally, because at least it shields you from being single. You choose to live your life at 70% of your full potential, but you cannot help hoping that things will change somewhere in the future.

We are thoroughly misled. It is true that things will turn out differently when you take responsibility and reach out. It won't necessarily be a success story from the moment you announce that you are going to start your own business. People will get upset if you are not following their well-intended advice to stay low anymore. You will potentially lose clients if you dare to ask more money than the value that you add. It is hard work if you want to upgrade your potential by even a small margin. It is a very uncertain path when you decide to take full responsibility. Then again, so is life. You might have built up all kinds of so-called certainties in your life, but every one of them can vanish tomorrow, without prior warning. One thing remains. You are guaranteed to be stuck in the uncertain status quo, living a mediocre life, if you don't take full accountability for your own mindset.

THE BUTTERFLY CIRCUS

This is my favorite short movie on unleashing potential. At the height of the Great Depression, the showman of a renowned circus discovers a man without limbs being exploited at a carnival sideshow. After an intriguing encounter with the showman, the limbless man is driven to hope for dreams and aspirations he had previously thought impossible.

thechangemindset.video/butterfly-circus

THE CHAN

The 'growth' mindset is a mindset that is open to change. Three crucial ingredients play an important role if you wish to stay agile and flexible in this world:

YES...   you need to suspend your judgement, break fixed thinking patterns and dream big

AND...   explore the world from a different perspective to generate new ideas

ACT...   on it because the key to real innovation is experimenting and failing fast, often and forward.

E MINDSET

The 'Yes And Act' Manifesto

The 'Yes And Act' manifesto is a declaration on how we see a world where creativity can flourish.

This manifesto will help people cope with the waves of change that are constantly occurring. The world is changing ever faster and it's happening everywhere. How do you perceive these waves of change? Are you a shipwreck survivor on a raft, or are you a surfer? A lot of people feel overwhelmed by the continuous waves of change. They try to resist them by sticking to their fixed thinking patterns. Alternatively, you could choose to become a 'change' surfer and develop skills to transform problems into opportunities. The 'Yes and Act' manifesto is for the change-surfers among us. Use it as a source of inspiration when you want to take the next step towards your own growth in your professional or personal life.

Link to download manifesto: https://cyrielkortleven.link/manifesto

YES

AVOID: YES, BUT... IT ALREADY EXISTS, OUR CUSTOMERS WON'T LIKE THAT, I'M NOT CREATIVE, THE MARKET IS NOT READY YET, IT'S TOO DIFFICULT, WE ARE TOO SMALL, NO BUDGET, LET'S BE REALISTIC, ETC...

NO IDEAKILLERS

KNOW THAT THE IMPOSSIBLE IS ONLY TEMPORARY

OUT OF THE BOX OR OUT OF BUSINESS?

BELIEVE 200% IN YOUR IDEAS **DREAM BIG**

SUSPEND JUDGEMENT START SMALL

EVERY PROBLEM CAN BE **TRANSFORMED** INTO AN OPPORTUNITY

DON'T GET STUCK IN THE TRAP OF MEDIOCRITY

DIVERGE AND

FIND A SECOND SOLUTION

AND A THIRD... AND A FOURTH... AND A FIFTH... AND A SIXTH... AND A SEVENTH... AND A THIRTIETH... AND A NINETY NINTH...

THE INTERESTING STUFF HAPPENS OUTSIDE YOUR COMFORTZONE TAKE A DIFFERENT PERSPECTIVE

THINK IN ALTERNATIVES

LOOK AROUND AND USE THE WEIRDEST OBJECT IN YOUR SIGHT AS INSPIRATION TO GET NEW IDEAS

WHAT IF? WHAT WOULD STEVE JOBS, GANDHI, SUPERMAN, A CHILD OF SIX OR YOUR NEIGHBOUR DO?

IMAGINE MAKE NEW ASSOCIATIONS!

BREAK, BURN OR BAN THE BOX

EXPLORE THE WORLD AND IMMERSE YOURSELF IN NEW CULTURES

ACT

A NEARLING IS A POSITIVE WORD FOR SOMETHING NEW THAT WAS DONE WITH THE RIGHT INTENTIONS, WHICH HAS NOT -YET- LED TO THE RIGHT RESULTS.

SHOW UP IN THE ARENA EVERYDAY

LIFE IS AN EXPERIMENT IT'S EASIER TO ASK FORGIVENESS

BECOME A PASSION-A-HOLIC **THAN IT'S TO ASK PERMISSION**

EXPLORE START ANYWHERE... JUST **START**. DARE TO STOP HAVE THE GUTS TO LET GO OF CONTROL

BE AMAZED GO FOR **NANO-IDEAS**. TAKE THE NEXT SMALL STEP

FAIL FAST, OFTEN AND FORWARD THERE'S ONLY ONE MOMENT TO DECIDE TO CHANGE YOUR LIFE. LIFE IS SHORT **NOW**

CHANGE THE WORLD (AND START WITH YOURSELF) **CHOOSE LIFE**

CREATED BY CYRIELKORTLEVEN.COM | DESIGN BY MISTIMAGES.BE   WWW.YESANDACT.COM

YES stands for positive thinking and suspending judgement. The self-fulfilling prophecy is working stronger than ever, and if you limit your own thoughts, you are effectively creating your own prison of limited reality. If you don't believe 200% in your own ideas, why should anybody else believe in them? So, dare to think big ... . No, even bigger! As Les Brown says, if you shoot for the moon and you miss, you will still land among the stars. Avoid the trap of mediocrity.

This is the situation where you want to follow your passion, but some less desirable option seems more feasible so, you choose that one instead. Be positive, and look at how you can transform a problem into an opportunity. Sometimes, just looking at the same situation from a different perspective is already enough to establish a mind shift. On to the big dreams- it's important to suspend judgement about change. We - human beings - don't like too much change, and your mind will instantly come up with all kinds of reasons as to why the status quo is better. For example: no time, no budget or it's too difficult. If your own mind doesn't come up with these idea-killers, then you can bet that people in your environment will throw them at you.

ACT is the most difficult part of the manifesto. It's about getting into action and experimenting with a lot of different solutions. If you're doing things in the domain of innovation and change, there is no certainty. Nobody knows whether a certain solution will work or not. There's only one way to find out: just do it. You will come across a lot of 'nearlings'. A nearling is a positive word for something new that was done with the right intentions, which has not led to the right result (yet). It is totally normal that things won't work perfectly at once.

Do you know of a child that learned to drive a bike without falling? No. Experiencing nearlings is inherently connected to change and innovation. Make sure that you can fail fast, often and forward. Have the guts to experiment and remember that it's easier to ask for forgiveness than to beg for permission. Success, in the long run, is for the people who show up to the arena every day. Those are the people who work very hard every day, for those who try new things. Sometimes it works and sometimes it doesn't, but they learn something new every day. So, go on ... step outside of your comfort zone and experiment. Take the first small step to see if you're going in the right direction.

AND

means exploring different views and stimulating your imagination. It is using all the creativity methods at your disposal to transform more ideas into action. Instead of experiencing the world from one point of view, switch your perspective. Remember the quote that says the most interesting stuff is happening outside your comfort zone.

Don't allow yourself to be satisfied with the first solution that comes to your mind. Look for a second solution, and a third... These alternatives will help you to make a better choice after you've suspended your judgement. Imagine how Steve Jobs, Mahatma Ghandi, Superman, or a child of six would solve your challenge. Make a list of 100 'what if' questions to broaden the scope of your question. Cross the borders of functions, departments, organisations or cultures to discover new opportunities.

FRANK DE WINNE

ASTRONAUT EUROPEAN SPACE AGENCY, BELGIUM'S SECOND PERSON IN SPACE, COMMANDER OF ISS EXPEDITION 21, 6 MONTHS SPACE, FOOTBALL, GASTRONOMY, HUSBAND, FATHER OF 3 CHILDREN, ...

Before a new group of astronauts go into space, they have a very long and profound training schedule ahead of them. A lot of the training is based on simulation and doing experiments - resembling possible situations that can happen in space. One important training element is CAVES. CAVES stands for Cooperative Adventure for Valuing and Exercising Human Behaviour and Performance Skills. This two-week course prepares astronauts to work safely and effectively in multicultural teams in an environment where safety is critical – in caves. Topics include leadership, teamwork, decision-making and problem-solving skills.

An important element of the expedition is the daily debriefing, which reflects on the successes and errors of the day, on similarities with spaceflight experiences; on how to reapply successful strategies as well as improving by learning from mistakes.

Image Credits: European Space Agency

OFF-NOMINALS

An "off nominal" is a term that they use in the space industry for something that isn't a standard procedure. An off nominal in space could be a fire, or an error in the software. You can't foresee a thing like this happening and you can only learn skills to stay flexible and agile whilst doing a lot of simulations to see how you can collaborate with your team in space and on earth to solve the problem. At ESA they do not only have a whole training program focused on these off nominals, but they are world-famous for their ESA Caves (Cooperative Adventure for Valuing and Exercising Human Behaviour and Performance Skills) training focused on developing skills in areas of leadership, teamwork, decision-making and problem-solving skills.

One example of an off-nominal happened to Frank while he was in space. He had to replace an old computer that was responsible for their freezers (where they store the scientific samples). To reduce the heat of those computers, they are stored on "cold plates" (a plate that keeps the computers cold by circulating cold water). Due to a technical error, the water started to pour out of the tube and began to float around in the air (remember, we're in space) - which is of course very dangerous because the whole room consists of technical materials, electricity ...

Frank immediately called his colleagues for support and the idea that popped into his head was to cover the tube with his body and T-shirt in an attempt to 'collect' as much water as possible whilst keeping it from floating. These are situations that you can't foresee, and for that reason it's so important to develop the right skills to think agile and don't panic.

THE BIG DREAM

Exploring space is of course one of the big dreams of most human beings. The possibility of discovering new stars, planets and maybe even extraterrestrial life is very intriguing.

It's not a big surprise that most employees in the space industry are incredibly motivated to realise this dream. It is also no surprise that the motivation, drive and pride is higher compared to a lot of other organisations in the benchmark. Questionnaire done with employees of ESA - European Space Agency.

Having a big dream will certainly help to engage and motivate people to go the extra step.

YES

Suspending your judgement is the first ingredient to allow change. Idea-killers (expressions like 'yes but...', 'we don't have money', 'we already tried it', ...) are the main reasons why change is so hard to accomplish. That doesn't mean that we shouldn't say 'no' anymore, but if the goal is to generate new ideas and allow change a chance, we have to postpone our judgement at some moments.

Combine this with a GIGA dream and we have the starting blocks for a successful change process. A good question to explore when you look for your Giga dream is 'What am I willing to struggle for?'

IDEA KILLERS...

REASONS WHY CREATIVITY AND INNOVATION DON'T FLY IN YOUR ORGANISATION

Yes, but... It already exists! Our customers won't like that!

WE DON'T HAVE TIME... **NO!** It's not possible...

It's too expensive! Let's be realistic... That's not logical...

We need to do more research... THERE'S NO BUDGET...

I'm not creative... We don't want to make mistakes...

The management won't agree... **GET REAL...**

It's not my responsibility... It's too difficult to master...

THAT'S TOO BIG A CHANGE. . .

The market is not ready yet... Let's keep it under consideration...

It is just like... The older generation will not use it...

WE ARE TOO SMALL FOR THAT...

It might work in other places but not here...

SINCE WHEN ARE YOU THE EXPERT?... That's for the future...

There are no staff members available...

IT IS NOT SUITABLE FOR OUR CLIENTS...

Poster from the book: Creativity in Business
Download your own poster at: www.ideakillers.net

WATCH OUT FOR ...

Human beings have a tendency to criticise and judge new things. This happens in a fraction of a second, where our brain looks at the new idea and compares it with previous experiences. If there's a big difference between the new idea and the thing our brain knows, it blocks the idea because it doesn't fit in the picture.

There are many (sometimes good) reasons why we do this: being afraid to go out of our comfort zone, or we only see the downside of the idea, we expect that the new idea will cost a lot of money, and will take a lot of time, ... We call all these reasons idea-killers. All kind of expressions that are meant to keep the status quo and make sure that we don't have to change.

THE YES BUT CHAIR

Daan Roosegaarde (Studio Roosegaarde) has developed the 'Yes, but'-chair. This chair has voice recognition and will give you a little shock when you say the words 'yes, but'. He developed this chair because he was frustrated that so many people start a response with these words when they first hear a new idea. Wouldn't it be great to have such chairs in every meeting room, when you're looking for more creativity?

THE FIRST IDEA-KILLERS

This is a short movie about a group of cavemen that are sitting in a focus group discussing the possibilities of the wheel. You will probably recognise a lot of behaviour that may happened earlier this week in your own meeting.

thechangemindset.video/inventionwheel

THE 3 MINUTE RULE

This exercise will help you double or triple the number of ideas that you'll come up with during a meeting (if you apply the exercise in the right way ;-)). You can download a poster with idea killers on www.ideakillers.net.

The 3-minute rule works as follows:

1. Select one item on the agenda you're going to apply the 3-minute rule to. In general, if you have a list of 10 agenda points, use your logical thinking and experience to make decisions for 9 of these agenda points. Most of the time, there's one agenda item that could use some additional creative thoughts. Pick that item and reformulate it into a creative question.

> *Note in case you're not familiar with the concept:*
>
> *A good creative question is concrete and challenging and starts with the words 'How can I/we ...'. E.g. if you want to attract more customers with a new product, a good creative question would be: 'How can we market our new product to double the number of customers in a month?'*

2. Invite your colleagues - for three minutes – to get into the 'yes, and' mindset. Instead of responding with an idea-killer to a new idea, they have to answer with 'yes, and ...'. This forces them to initially accept the idea and add something to it. It might be very interesting to put a print of the idea killer poster on the table before you start.

3. During the 3 minutes, no judgement is allowed and quantity of reactions is more important than quality at that moment. If somebody in the group is still using an idea-killer, the other group members can point to the idea-killers poster to make the person aware that he or she used an idea-killer. The punishment for this is that the idea-killing person must come up with 2 new ideas because they killed one idea. Quite often this judgement happens in an unconscious way, so the person isn't aware that he or she was destroying an idea. It is in fact, an awareness exercise.

4. You will notice that after three minutes, you will have a lot more ideas than in a normal set-up. Also, you'll probably get some crazy ideas. That is NOT a problem because you don't have to implement all of them. Make sure that everybody can see the ideas (maybe put post-its on the table or use a flipchart to write the ideas down).

5. Select the ideas or (importantly) a part of an idea that might be feasible or interesting and combine different small ideas to one or two bigger ones. Those are the ideas that you are going to test.

"The one who says it cannot be done should never interrupt the one who is doing it."

Anonymous

Advantages of the '3 minute rule':

+ You will generate a lot more ideas than in a normal discussion

+ You will also allow the crazier ideas to the table, which might result in a breakthrough

+ You give everybody a chance to contribute

+ There's a good chance that some of the ideas will be implemented because people feel responsible for them (since they had a chance to contribute)

+ It only takes 3 minutes (so even if you don't find a good idea, there wasn't any significant time 'wasted').

IDEA BOOSTERS...

THE ATTITUDE TO BOOST CREATIVITY AND INNOVATION IN YOUR ORGANISATION

Yes, and... Let's find the concept behind it...

Wow, interesting... **YES!** Maybe now is the right time...

You are on to something... **Good, let's enrich the idea...**

How do they do this in other industries?... Tell me more...

Let's look at the financials later... Let's ship!

Our industry is ready for disruption... **Let's experiment...**

Great! LET'S MAKE IT EVEN MORE CONCRETE...

It's time for change... I will try it tomorrow with one client...

What's the worst thing that could happen?... What are we waiting for?...

WHAT IF A COMPETITOR WOULD STEAL THIS IDEA?...

I love you! Let's spend the lunchtime on it today...

Convince me in 3 minutes... I feel the potential... Why the hell not...

Find a problem... **Fix it...** Start a company...

Stop discussing... Start doing!

LET'S KICKSTART THIS PROJECT!

Poster from the book: Creativity in Business
Download your own poster at: www.ideaboosters.net

There's also a poster with idea-boosters available. Put both posters in your meeting room and refer to them when you want to generate some new ideas.
www.ideaboosters.net

NO IS ALSO OKAY

Do I need to change my life now?

NO! Do a kind of emotional check to gauge if you're happy or unhappy with your life. If the balance is towards the happy side, keep on doing what you do. Only change the (parts of) your life where you are no longer satisfied with the current situation.

Will change be easy?

NO! Change is not easy. It's f*cking hard work. If it were easy, then everybody would already have changed their bad habits.

Should I always say 'Yes, And'

NO! 95% of the time, use your logical thinking and common sense. Only use 'Yes, And' if you want to change something, and need some creative ideas

Do I need to be happy all the time?

NO! Life has its ups and downs. Happiness is an emotion and emotions are not stable: they come and go. Allow the emotions that are present at this moment. Happiness is not a mathematical equation. Focus on what's meaningful for you instead of pursuing happiness

Am I a real, unique person in this world?

NO! There are probably thousands (maybe millions) of people who have similar skills to you, and there's a good chance that a lot of them are better than you. If everybody were extraordinary, this would immediately mean that nobody is extraordinary. Most of your actions will be 'boring' and unnoteworthy, but that's totally okay. We always think that we need to be extraordinary to live a great life, but if you appreciate the small things in life - the things you already have -, you already have a lot that matters

BECOME A KNIGHT OF NO

It may sound like a contradiction, but you need to combine saying 'No' with the 'Yes, And' skill if you really want to achieve your big dream.

When you say yes to something, it's imperative that you understand what you're saying no to. Now and again, we all struggle with saying no, because you want to be helpful, you want to avoid being rude, or you are afraid of conflict or missed opportunities. But life is too short to do everything, and you can't please everyone. If you want to accomplish big things that are meaningful (this can be anything - earning a lot of money, starting an orphanage in Africa or designing a beautiful artwork), you have to become a 'knight who says no'.

STEVE JOBS WAS ONE OF THE MASTER KNIGHTS

who reduced the number of Apple products from 350 to 10 within a year, when he returned to Apple. He formulated this to perfection: "People think focus means saying yes to the thing you've got to focus on. But that's not what it means at all. It means saying no to the hundreds of other good ideas that there are. You have to pick carefully. I'm actually as proud of the things we haven't done as the things I have done. Innovation is saying no to 1,000 things."

The simplest and most direct way is just saying 'No I can't or don't want to' in a respectful and clear way, but here are two alternatives if you don't want to give a 'clear no': 'I'm not the best person to be of assistance in this. Why don't you try X' or 'let me think about it first and I'll get back to you within X amount of time (and of course give your honest reply within the time-limit)'.

A 'no' uttered from the deepest conviction is better than a 'yes' merely uttered to please, or worse, to avoid trouble. - Mahatma Gandhi

XAVIER MAASSEN

PROFESSIONAL RACING DRIVER, GT RACING, CONSCIOUSNESS COACH, SPORTSMARKETING, QUALITY, EFFICIENCY, ENDURANCE RACING, EXPOSURE, BRAND ACTIVATION, NETWORKING, PASSION.

Pictures © Brecht Decancq

WINNING 24 HOURS OF LE MANS

My biggest dream and ambition is to win the 24 Hours of Le Mans. This is the world's oldest active sportscar race in endurance racing. I've been on the podium once, the first year I went to the 24 Hours of Le Mans. It's the biggest and most beautiful race in the world and my ambition is definitely to win the race. Three years ago, we had a good chance to get on the podium again, due to technical trouble in advance we had to start with a penalty and knew that we wouldn't make a chance to win the race that year. I was really 'pissed' because winning at Le Mans is one of my big dreams. But I could change my mindset by thinking about all the little kids who would love to be part of this race (like I did many years ago) and look at me ... I'm part of the race. Thanks to those thoughts I could switch my anger into gratefulness and I have enjoyed every moment of the race.

EXPERIMENT, FAIL AND LEARN.

We are always trying new things because winning or losing a race is often a fraction of seconds. The nice thing about experimenting in racing is that you see the results immediately. If the stopwatch shows your time is better than your previous lap then you know you're quicker. It's quite logical that you experiment in the free practice laps and you don't change major things during qualifying or the race itself. But you always have to be at the edge in this profession. That requires experimenting, sometimes failing and learning from those failures.

WINNING IS ALSO A MINDSET

A few years ago, I had a really important race where I could take the lead in the championship. My biggest opponent was out of the race, we were leading but we had to go for a pitstop. But something went wrong and I came back in fourth position, more than 14 seconds behind the number one in the race. At that moment I was really disappointed and I was in a very negative mindset. I was mad at my team who made a mistake and I was looking at all kinds of external factors that I couldn't influence. At that moment, I made a conscious decision to transfer my anger and energy into something positive and use it to be totally focused on getting the win this race.

I passed the first car and it was a constant struggle between my positive thoughts and the negative emotions that I would never win this race. But I managed to also pass number two and my last opponent was still 7 seconds ahead of me. I tried to focus completely on my driving and hoped that he would make a mistake. I kept on pushing & pushing and by the last lap, I was two seconds behind him. Which is still not enough to win the race but i didn't want to give up because I had already won almost 12 seconds back.

I kept the thought in my mind that seeing the finish line is not yet crossing the finish line. We were at three or four corners before the end of the race and he made a mistake - probably feeling the tension that I was getting closer and closer. I came right behind him and it was still three corners away. I couldn't pass him on these corners but I got a better exit out of the last corner on to the main straight. I got up next to him, he pushed my car in the grass and I was two wheels in the grass and we both went over the finish line.

I won that race with six thousands of a second and it was absolutely one of my most incredible wins. It proved to me that it's so easy to blame external conditions or give up early- but if you can make a conscious mind shift and stay persistent, impossible goals might sometimes get reality. And maybe you don't always win but if you give up, you know for sure that you will not make it, so always go flat-out for your impossible dreams.

GIGA

A GIGA DREAM CONSIST OF 3 THINGS

1. NO LIMITS
2. VISUALISE THE FINISH LINE
3. GIVES ENERGY

1. NO LIMITS

The Giga dream is a synonym for a BHAG. Jim Collins & Jerry Porras (author of the book Built to Last) introduces the acronym BHAG (pronounced bee-hag) which is short for 'Big, Hairy Audacious Goals'. These are extremely bold objectives to which great organisations commit utterly and completely. BHAGS are so ambitious that they often seem unrealistic, especially to outsiders. Nevertheless, they are also clear and tangible enough to energise and focus the organisation.

A well-known example of a non-corporate Giga dream is the one set by John F. Kennedy in 1961 when he proclaimed 'that this nation should commit itself to achieving the goal, before this decade is out, of landing a man on the moon and returning him safely to earth.' This was a very bold commitment at the time.

The translation from a Giga dream into SMART (specific, measurable, achievable, relevant and time-related) goals is important, but it's the second phase. The whole purpose of a Giga dream is to stretch your limits and go out of your comfort zone. Dare to explore the borders of the impossible.

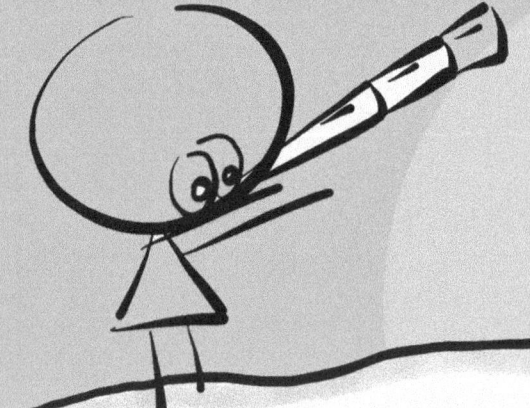

2. VISUALISE THE FINISH LINE

It is not a lack of resources that holds people back, rather a lack of resourcefulness. To end your Giga dream visualise what is possible in the future, rather than being stuck in the present. Look at things not as they are now, but as they can be – without constraints.

Use visualisation as a kind of mental rehearsal, which gives you a compelling taste of what your vision will be like in reality. How do you know when you've realised your Giga dream? What do you see? What do you hear? What kind of feelings will you have in your belly? Create a mental picture of the 'finish line' to make the Giga dream concrete. Having a huge, compelling Giga dream doesn't mean that it's vague or unclear. It is tangible, energising, highly focused. People "get it" right away; it takes little or no explanation.

3. GIVES ENERGY

You will know if you've found your Giga dream because you can feel the energy in your whole body. It will engage people; it reaches out and grabs them in the gut. You will find it stimulating, exciting and adventurous. It will stimulate forward progress and momentum. You will want to throw in your creative talents, and skills to go for it.

A Giga dream differs quite a lot from the meaningless, impossible to remember mission statements that a lot of companies are using. Most mission statements are ambitious, but they often consist of very vague terms and lack the energy required to engage their people to take action.

Built to Last by Jim Collins & Jerry Porras

BELIEVE IN YOUR GIGA DREAMS

In 1986, a football team lived on a little island in the south of Thailand called "Koh Panyee". It's a floating village in the middle of the sea that has not an inch of soil. The kids here loved to watch football, but had nowhere to play or practice. However, they didn't let that stop them. They challenged the norm and have become a great inspiration for new generations on the island.

thechangemindset.video/gigadream

Everybody would enjoy the applause after they have finished a marathon, but are they willing to run several hours a week by themselves (when it's raining and they have other things to do), in order to get there?

Everybody would like to earn a million a year, but are they prepared to work 60 hours a week for it?

Everybody dreams of having an amazing relationship, but are they ready to have the tough conversations, and to experience the emotional turbulence that comes with it?

Most people fall in love with an imagined end-result, but forget that there is a (long and often hard) process to get to that result. This means that 'What do you want out of life?' is not the right question to define your big dream in life. A better question would be:

WHAT ARE YOU WILLING TO STRUGGLE FOR?

People who dared to dream Giga and took action:

Pythagoras, Jimmy Wales, Oprah Winfrey, Galileo, Elon Musk, Albert Einstein, Aristotle, Jack Ma, Nelson Mandela, Shakespeare, Margaret Fuller, Charles Darwin, Marie Curie, Ghandi, Joan of Arc, Descartes, Steve Jobs, Cleopatra, Wright Brothers, Isaac Newton, Louis Pasteur, Queen Anne, Thomas Alva Edsion, Max Planck, Mother Theresa, Plato, Benjamin Franklin, Copernicus, Alexander Graham Bell, Alfred Nobel, Florence Nightingale, Thomas Graham, Michael Faraday, Blaise Pascal, Jane Austen, Henry Cavendish, Alessandro Volta, Wilhelm Conrad Rontgen, Martin Luther King, Emily Dickinson, Mark Zuckenberg, Paul Dirac, Neils Bohr, Sigmund Freud, Christopher Columbus, Antoine Laurent Lavoisier, Johannes Kepler, Billie Jean King, James Clerk Maxwell, Franz Boas, Linus Pauling, Edwin Hubble, Larry Page, Helen Keller, Joseph J Thompson, Stephen Hawking, Archimedes, Chien-shiung Wu, G Marconi, James Watt, Jane Goodall, Nikola Tesla, ...

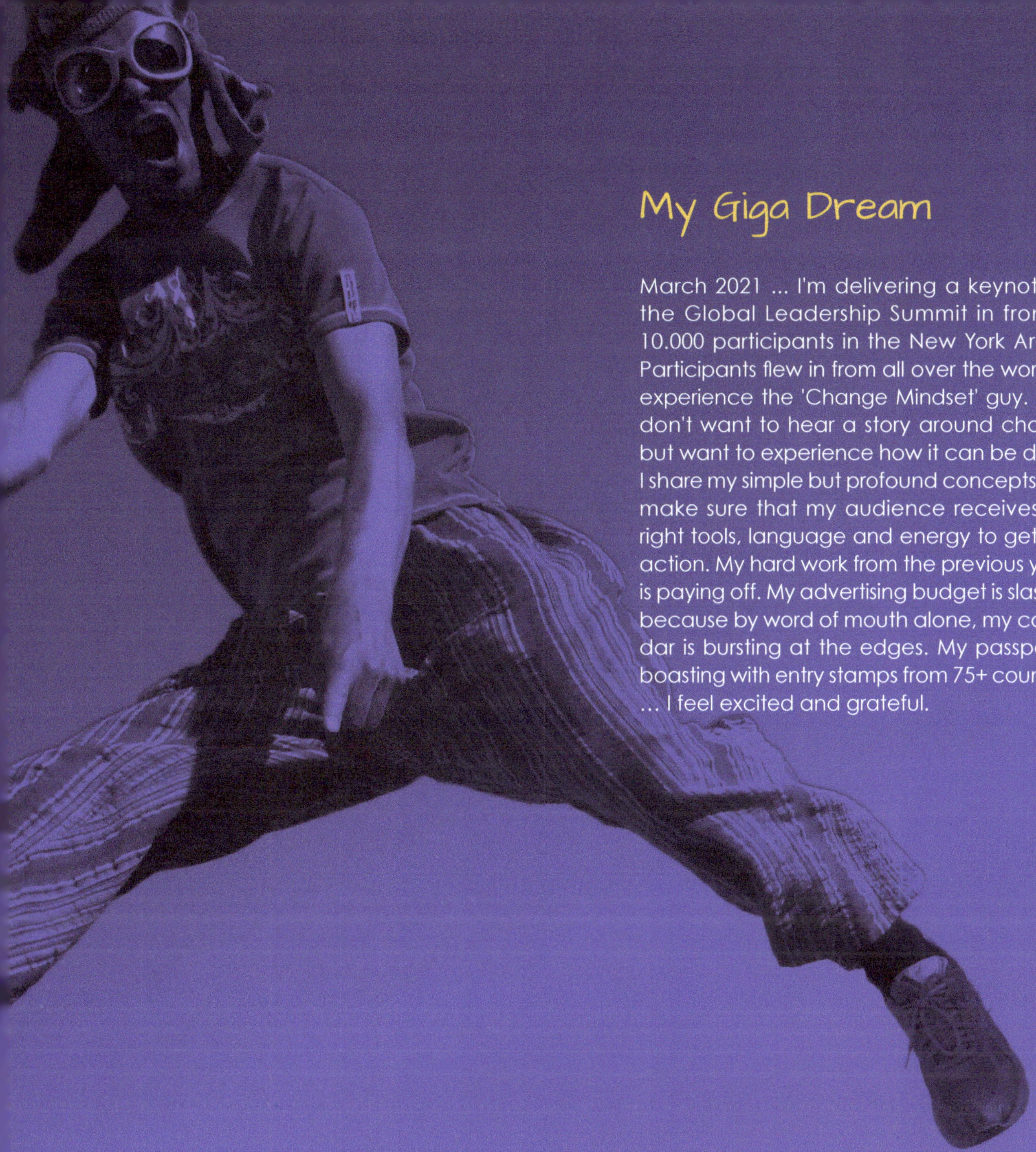

My Giga Dream

March 2021 … I'm delivering a keynote at the Global Leadership Summit in front of 10.000 participants in the New York Arena. Participants flew in from all over the world to experience the 'Change Mindset' guy. They don't want to hear a story around change but want to experience how it can be done. I share my simple but profound concepts and make sure that my audience receives the right tools, language and energy to get into action. My hard work from the previous years is paying off. My advertising budget is slashed because by word of mouth alone, my calendar is bursting at the edges. My passport is boasting with entry stamps from 75+ countries … I feel excited and grateful.

What kind of pain you are willing to suffer to realise your dream? For 99% of human beings (and 1% are the exceptions), it's damn hard work to realise one's dreams.

Does this mean that you shouldn't strive to go for your dreams? The opposite is true. You should go for it even with more energy and persistence, because it's absolutely worth going 100% full in. Be aware though, that it won't be an easy path.

*The sublte art of not giving a f*ck by Mark Manson*

People who are very good at realising their big dreams often experience that they enjoy the road even more than the goal. They see the difficulties on the path as challenges, and feel excited every time they overcome another obstacle. Every obstacle or failure is a new lesson and one step closer to the goal. If you want to know how you can achieve your big dreams, check out the section around nano-steps in the ACT-chapter.

AND

Switching perspectives is a great way to broaden your own reality. The world can be experienced in many varieties & shapes.

If you can flip your perspective from a problem to an opportunity, suddenly many 'realities' are possible. Several creative methods will help you to generate hundreds of ideas in a short amount of time.

Inspired by the artwork of a Swiss artist Markus Raetz, I've created a 3D printed version of a Yes-No artwork. If you look from one perspective, you see the word 'No' but if you switch your position, you see the word 'Yes'. The artwork hasn't changed, you have altered your viewpoint.

This seemingly simple artwork is an essential ingredient of having a change mindset. It allows you to switch from a 'negative' perspective that you don't like anymore to a more 'positive' perspective.

SWITCHING PERSPECTIVE

Imagine that you have one client who is always complaining. He calls you every week to tell you what is wrong with your service. Everybody in the office already knows about him, they recognise his phone number and try to avoid being the one that picks up the phone. most colleagues consider this person a problem-client. If you are able to look from a different perspective to this situation, you could also see a person that contacts you weekly to give you feedback on how to improve your service. It's somebody who takes the effort to pick up the phone and spend time to explain why certain elements could be better if applied in a different way.

Chances are that a lot of the 'issues' that come up may be irrelevant for you, or difficult to solve but it is also possible that once in a while, that person comes up with a great idea to improve your service. It might help you to create more happy clients. The danger is -if we have given that person the perspectives of 'NO' or 'Problem', we don't see or hear the potential of certain remarks anymore. Everything that person says, immediately goes into the imaginary 'rubbish bin'. As a result, you might miss out on some great opportunities.

The fact that we can switch perspectives (you

have just proven that you are capable of it, because you could see a 'No' and a 'Yes' in the artwork mentioned before) means that reality is not always what it seems to be.

Reality plays tricks on our creativity by only allowing us to see what there is. If we take this one step further, we can only see what we think is there. So, we get 'used' to our own perspective of reality. Studies have already proven that perception consists of information gathered from outside for only 20%. Consequently, 80% is produced in the brain itself. All our senses pick up information from the outside world and transform that into an image inside our head. For that reason, our society (politics, advertising, ...) puts a lot of - sometimes unintended - effort into influencing our reality. The patterns that we are seeing are not coming from the outside but are rooted in our own perceptions.

Rodolfo Llinas, a professor of neurology at the medical faculty of New York University goes a step further and claims that the outside world is just a projection created by our brains. A motion picture that explores the endless possibilities of this is 'Inception' by Christopher Nolan. In the movie, layer upon layer of brain projections are created in order to effectively alter someone's reality.

WHAT'S YOUR PERSPECTIVE ON LIFE?

No... Yes... Problem...
Opportunity...

thechangemindset.video/yesno

The thinking patterns that influence our perception are the reason why switching to a new perspective is hard to do. It took hundreds of years before humanity accepted to switch the perspective from a flat to a round earth.

If you want to change, you need to do that effectively, otherwise you will always be thinking that the status quo (or old ways of thinking) are preferable. If you still believe that your old phone is better than a smartphone, then chances are you're still using your old phone. If you believe that to command and control is the best way to manage your employees, you will never make the switch to self-steering teams, because it doesn't fit in your perspective, which is your reality.

If you believe that self-driving cars; artificial intelligence and 3D printing are dangerous inventions, then you won't experiment or use these new technologies until the moment arrives when your perspective switches - the reason for the change of perspective can have all kind of circumstances.

The above examples prove that it is truly possible to change your own perspective and look from a different angle at a situation. This means that you can make a decision to at least try and explore new pathways to solve a certain challenge.

A E I F U

WHICH SYMBOL DOESN'T BELONG IN THIS ROW?

You probably answered 'F' because it is not a vowel. And you're right. That is a correct answer. Hmmm, 'a' correct answer? Why isn't it 'the' correct answer? Well, maybe you notice that the 'U' is the only one that has a curve in it, all other letters have straight lines. This means that 'U' is also a correct answer to this question. Wait a minute ... couldn't 'A' also be a correct answer because it's the only one that has a closed triangle in its shape?

We can continue like this until you've found several reasons why a certain letter doesn't belong in that row. This is already an example of switching perspectives in action. However, it is possible to take it to the next level. In my question, I use the word 'symbols' on purpose instead of letters. You're probably still looking at these symbols as letters of the alphabet. You're correct again. These symbols are also letters of the alphabet, but what else could they be? What happens if you switch your perspective and describe these symbols as objects that you can use in your house?

The first symbol 'A' might be perceived in your brain as a ladder. The 'U' could become a glass. The 'E' is maybe part of a comb or a rake. Suddenly new solutions appear and the only thing that you have done is switched your perspective from letters of the alphabet to objects around your house.

The funny thing is that it happens right in front of your eyes. It happens in an instant. During one

A story has different angles

thechangemindset.video/differentangle

The mysterious symbol of the monks

thechangemindset.video/mysterious-symbol

of my presentations, one participant said that the second symbol looked like a parking space where you can park two cars. From the moment she gave this answer, suddenly the whole room started to laugh.

The reason was that the answer was quite unexpected, and our brains released endorphins (brain chemicals for the feel-good effect). At the same moment, everybody in the room could 'perceive' this weird comment as a valid answer. The range of possibilities had expanded, and the collective perception had changed.

Here's to those who have always seen things differently

The colour changing card trick from Richard Wiseman

thechangemindset.video/apple-different

thechangemindset.video/colourchangingcardtrick

21 ACTIVITIES TO BROADEN YOUR PERSPECTIVE

There are lots of options to broaden your perspective and view on the world. Travelling to a different country is a brilliant one because you have to get out of your comfort zone on many levels (you will experience a different environment, culture, food, local habits, ...).

But how can you broaden your perspective on a 'normal' working day?

GO TO THE LOCAL GROCERY STORE AND BUY ONE PIECE OF FRUIT & ONE TYPE OF VEGETABLE THAT YOU'VE NEVER TASTED BEFORE (AND TRY IT OF COURSE).

DRINK SOMETHING ELSE INSTEAD OF YOUR NORMAL COFFEE OR TEA FOR BREAKFAST (OKAY YOU CAN START WITH A COFFEE, SOME HABITS SHOULDN'T BE CHANGED).

SWITCH FOR 2 HOURS TO A DIFFERENT RADIO -STATION (OR UNKNOWN SPOTIFY LIST).

LEAVE A SHORT NOTE (CREATIVE PEO-PLE CAN WRITE A SHORT POEM) TO THANK THE MAILMAN OR THE CLEANER.

ANSWER EVERY QUESTION THAT YOU GET TODAY WITH ANOTHER QUESTION.

TAKE AT LEAST ONE INTUITIVE DECISION TODAY (WITHOUT ANALYZING YOUR DECISION).

ALLOW YOURSELF A GIFT AND BUY A NEW BOOK IN THE BOOK-STORE (IN A DIFFER-ENT WRITING GENRE THAN WHAT YOU NORMALLY READ).

END YOUR DAY WITH A GLASS OF CHAMPAGNE AND LOOK BACK AT THE BEAUTIFUL THINGS THAT HAVE HAPPENED TODAY.

ASK 3 STRANGERS ABOUT THEIR BIG DREAM IN LIFE.

GO TO YOUTUBE AND TYPE IN THE KEYWORDS OF A PROFESSIONAL CHALLENGE THAT YOU'RE FACING AT THIS MOMENT (AND PUT A TIMER OF 21 MINUTES TO MAKE SURE THAT YOU RETURN TO YOUR NORMAL ACTIVITIES).

PLAN ONE HOUR 'NETWORKING' IN YOUR AGENDA AND GO UP OR DOWN ONE LEVEL IN THE BUILDING AND CONNECT WITH SOME NEW COLLEAGUES/ ORGANISATIONS (NEXT BUILDING IS ALSO FINE).

SKIP TWO PLANNED MEETINGS THIS WEEK AND ATTEND A MEETING FROM A DIFFERENT DEPARTMENT.

SPEND 10 MINUTES WATCHING A GROUP OF CHILDREN AT A PLAYGROUND.

START YOUR DAY WITH A GLASS OF CHAMPAGNE AND WISH YOURSELF A BRILLIANT DAY.

GET SOME COFFEE/TEA/OTHER DRINK FOR 3 COLLEAGUES THAT YOU DON'T KNOW VERY WELL.

TAKE A PIECE OF PAPER AND WRITE DOWN 21 QUESTIONS AROUND A BIG PROFESSIONAL CHALLENGE. YOU HAVE 7 MINUTES TO COMPLETE THIS TASK.

SHOW THIS PAGE TO THE PERSON WHO'S CLOSE IN YOUR NEIGHBOURHOOD RIGHT NOW AND ASK THAT PERSON WHAT (S)HE WOULD DO TO BROADEN THEIR PERSPECTIVE.

O TO A RESTAURANT AND RDER EXACTLY THE SAME HAT A PREVIOUS (UNNOWN) CLIENT ORDERED.

HAVE A CHAT WITH A COLLEAGUE THAT YOU DON'T KNOW VERY WELL ABOUT HIS/HER HOBBIES.

SHARE A NEARLING WITH YOUR PARTNER (YOU CAN FIND THE DEFINITION OF A NEARLING IN THE ACT CHAPTER).

HAVE LUNCH WITH A COLLEAGUE THAT YOU HAVEN'T SPOKEN IN THE LAST MONTH.

LOOKING FROM A DIFFERENT PERSPECTIVE: REALITY CHECK

The early adopters

"At bol.com many people are working according to the Spark-method (i.e. an adapted version of the holacracy model where the organisation is purpose driven & employees work in autonomous teams). It all started a few years ago when Harm Jans - who worked as a team leader in bol.com's logistics department - was inspired by the method. He decided to start with a pilot of two smaller teams. Harm collaborated with an experienced facilitator to deliver a kind of taster workshop where they explained the principles of the holacracy method and started with a group of enthusiastic employees. This group got a more extensive training and asked them for feedback. They liked several elements of the method and their work efficiency improved. They were the early adopters and as such extremely important to kick off a major change project in an organisation.

Thanks to the enthusiastic responses of the early adopters, we received questions from other teams how to apply some of the principles in their own team. A few people of top-management also heard what we were doing and at a certain moment the CEO noticed the incredible enthusiasm of the team-members involved. His involvement obviously gave a big boost to the whole project; suddenly we had sponsorship from top-management."

Main lessons:

- Choose your early adopters carefully because it is very hard to start a new change initiative if the first attempt fails.
- As an initiator, be open to feedback from the early adopters because that will actively engage them and they will take ownership of the change.
- Having sponsorship from the top is necessary to keep the ball running and make sure the whole project can grow in a sustainable way. At this moment 1.000 people (around 120 teams) at bol.com are applying the Spark method."

Harm Jans - Way of working lead @ Bol.com

Inspiration from outside

"Within EPAM, we want to stimulate our employees to think beyond their daily job. We have created dedicated rooms, which we call EPAM garages, where employees can experiment with new technologies and software. Next to the working table, tennis tables and playstations that we have, our engineers can actually build new software and products that we don't necessarily need or use within EPAM. Nevertheless the engagement level of our people increases and in some cases, we even financially support the development of some products even though we know that they will not become an EPAM product or service. Some people have started their own companies based on experiments in the garage.

Another way to integrate inspiration from outside is the organisation of several events. Our largest event is called the Software Engineering Conference where 3000 engineers and clients from all over the world gather. The event is broadcasted to all EPAM locations. Everyone within EPAM can submit an application for a story and some of them get on stage to share their insights and the projects they are working on.

Next to those big events, we organise several hackathons where we work 24 hours on specific projects to solve a very challenging problem. People can also organise their own meet-ups with colleagues from different departments around a specific technology challenge. You announce that you're doing such a meetup and people can register to attend it. Most of the time 10 to 15 people from different departments show up. EPAM provides some structure, such as locations and digital platforms to organise it, but 90% of these projects are initiated by enthusiastic employees."

Zoltan Szeni - Global HR Executive @ EPAM

Creating diverse teams

"We see a difference in mindset, thinking patterns and values between our millennials and our older managing directors. In general, the millennials are more creative and value flexible work arrangements and good equipment over a high salary.

What works exceptionally well for us is that we mix the different groups (managing directors, millennials and even people from our talent pool) and let them work together in design thinking sessions. These diverse teams create a mindset where people can look at the world from different perspectives and respect those different views."

Simone Wamsteker – HR Service Delivery Lead @ Accenture

CHRIS BARTLETT

HUMAN RESOURCES LIAISON TO PUBLIC AFFAIRS, LABOR RELATIONS AND SUSTAINABILITY @ UPS, PASSIONATE ADVOCATE FOR POWER OF CONVERSATION AND GAMING, INTERPERSONAL AND MASS COMMUNICATION.

FAST PROTOTYPING FOR OUR NEW STRATEGY

Instead of sitting in a room with a small group of people trying to come up with the perfect strategy, we applied a lot of fast prototyping. When developing a new strategy, it's likely that there's only a small group of people who can grasp acomplete overview of all the pieces. While it's not necessary that everybody understand everything at the start, you still want to have a process that allows people to learn as you go. Fast prototyping chops the whole into smaller chunks, and then those chunks are used an reviewed by the whole team in iterative steps. As everyone works on these pieces, the development process itself works to lift the whole team's understanding.

This process also help when it comes to diverse audience outreach. Communicating the strategy requires that the message make sense to the different kinds of receivers. Fast prototyping gave us a head start, as people with different jobs and strengths have already reacted to the pieces as they were created. Then, as soon as soon as we had a first draft, we literally took somebody from the management team to one of our first-line teams, to check if the strategy made sense to them.

We repeated this 'reality check' all along the process – develop a draft, review it with the team, and get it to the first-line management team as quickly as was feasible. Rapid prototyping created a meaningful feedback loop that rotated at a very quick pace. We're quite sure the whole communication went faster than a normal top-down communication strategy because there was less confusion. People felt more engaged because they had a chance to contribute something to the strategy. Of course, not everybody agreed with the strategy, but at least it was clear in which direction we were going.

COMMUNICATING A NEW STRATEGY TO 400.000 EMPLOYEES

Translating a new strategy from the board to the rest of the company is always a challenge. If your company is UPS, and you have more than 400,000 employees working all over the world, I would call it a huge challenge. We made use of a lot of visual tools - an illustrated approach meant we relied less on the written word,

This was a great help in managing culture and language differences in our global company. We still had to adapt some of the visuals depending on which country we were approaching but it made for a more powerful, more engaging deliverable.

Another piece we put into play was a board game. We actually took our management team at all levels and all countriesthrough a board game that basically took our strategy and rewarded you for following the strategy.

A big part of the success of the game was the fact that we put the upper-level management teams at the same table as our first-linemanagement team. That environment led to a good translation of the strategy. Our frontline people don't need the same level of understanding of the strategy as middle or top-management, but they need to understand the impact of that strategy in their daily jobs.

We also created a comic strip with different characters, so that our people can see themselves in a different way. In the comic strip we reflected again the kind of behaviour that we would like to see from our people. at me ... I'm part of the race. Thanks to those thoughts I could switch my anger into gratefulness and I have enjoyed every moment of the race.

FAILURE IS PART OF THE PROCESS

Being able to experiment (and accept some failures) is essential within UPS to move forward. If we can prototype something and experiment with it in reality, that's a lot better than creating the perfect strategy on paper. During the whole communication process of the new strategy, a lot of the techniques didn't work and there was a whole graveyard of dead ideas that were eliminated during the process.

7 CREATIV METHOD

To make this part more concrete, we will introduce a very concrete challenge which we'll use to generate some ideas while applying the creativity methods:

How can I stimulate the creativity of my colleagues?

You'll find examples to solve this challenge below the method.

1. BRAINWRITING

1. All participants get a blank piece of paper + a marker
2. Give them 3 minutes to come up with at least 7 new ideas
3. When time's up, give your paper with ideas to the person on their right (every participant gets a 'new' paper with ideas from their neighbour)
4. Continue the process and try to generate 7 extra ideas - inspired by the ideas from your neighbour (build on the idea of your neighbour but write every idea down as a stand-alone idea)
5. Repeat this process one more round (this time share the paper with a neighbour 2 positions to the right)

Example: start with writing your own ideas on the paper. In the next round, you'll receive the paper from your neighbour and one of the ideas is 'Put posters with a motivational quote at the entrance.' Maybe you'll get inspired by that idea and build further on it and write down 'Create some template-posters with a challenging question like 'What's your biggest dream' and invite colleagues to write down their answer' or 'Ask 5 colleagues about their favorite quote and have a conversation around that quote.'

2. MAC GUYVER METHOD

MacGuyver was a very inventive secret agent in the homonymous TVseries. He always carried a Swiss army knife & duct-tape and he always found a clever solution based on the available resources when he was locked up somewhere. For this method, we also use 'random stimuli' to generate new ideas.

1. Let the participants form pairs + give them post-its + marker
2. The pairs walk around in the room (or outside) and 1 person points to a random object
3. The participants form a number of associations around that object
4. Re-associate - connect one of the associations back to the original challenge

Example: You walk with a participant outside and she points to a statue of the founder of the company. Use 'statue' as an object and come up with a few associations: stone, formal, respect, pedestal. Then write your new ideas on post-it notes starting from the associations. 'Formal' can lead to an idea like 'We create a formal procedure that every employee has to generate 3 ideas a day'; or 'Respect' can be transformed into an idea like 'People who share their ideas with colleagues will get more respect'.

3. PRESUPPOSITIONS

Method A
1. Select crucial terms in the starting formulation
2. Determine the presupposition in each of those terms
3. For each presupposition, ask the question 'What if this was not true?'
4. Re-associate - come up with new ideas

Method B
1. Write down the common characteristics of ideas in earlier rounds (these indicate presuppositions)
2. For each presupposition, ask the question 'What if this was not true?'
3. Resociate - come up with new ideas

Example method A: crucial terms are 'teamleader', 'stimulate', 'creativity' and 'colleagues'. Take the first term and rephrase the question - what if the teamleader wasn't responsible for stimulating the creativity. What kind of ideas would come up in that situation? Possible idea: we create a system of buddies where team members stimulate each other to be more creative.

Example method B: you might discover that a lot of ideas go in the direction of giving rewards or appraisal. What would happen if we can't give a positive reward. Possible idea: if you don't come up with 5 ideas/month, your salary will be lowered by 5%.

X FUNCTION

1. Marketing
2. Finance
3. Logistics
4. Human Resources
5. Health & Safety
6. Production
7. R&D
8. IT
9. Communication
10. Accounting
11. Customer service
12. Administration
13. Legal
14. Foreman
15. Quality control
16. Sales
...

X INDUSTRY

1. Automotive
2. IT
3. Retail
4. Government
5. Agriculture
6. Construction
7. Fashion
8. Healthcare
9. Banking
10. Entertainment
11. Communication
12. Transport
13. Pharmaceutical
14. Sports
15. Oil & Gas
16. Gaming
...

X ORGANISATION

1. Google
2. Disney
3. Coca cola
4. Federal government
5. Ikea
6. Ebay
7. Mac Donalds
8. DHL
9. Air Asia
10. MTV
11. Louis Vuiton
12. Facebook
13. Colgate
14. Red Bull
15. Nike
16. Spotify
...

X CULTURE

1. Belgium
2. Italy
3. Australia
4. China
5. America
6. India
7. South Africa
8. Sweden
9. Singapore
10. New Zealand
11. UK
12. Spain
13. Canada
14. Mexico
15. Botswana
16. Afghanistan
...

X RANDOM

1. Public speaker
2. your first love
3. Opera singer
4. Harvard prof
5. Arnold Schwarzenegger
6. your neighbour
7. Teenager
8. Kung fu master
9. Grumpy granddad
10. Harley biker
11. street artist
12. bartender
13. Tattoo artist
14. surfer dude
15. Toddler
16. your worst enemy
...

NOT INVENTED HERE
cross-industry innovation

RAMON VULLINGS & MARC HELEVEN

Ramon Vullings & Marc Heleven have written a book around cross industry innovation. Where can a hospital apply principles from the airline sector? How can a car manufacturer use tools from the video game industry? What can an event organiser learn from the railways?

Not invented here - Cross Industry Innovation by Ramon Vullings & Marc Heleven

"Don't think outside the box, think outside your industry."

Ramon Vullings

4. CROSSING BORDERS

1. Let the participants form pairs + give them some post-its + marker

2. Use the 'Crossing borders' sheet (next page) as inspiration.

3. You start with column 1 and one participant chooses a number between 1 and 16 - then you use the function that corresponds with that number as inspiration - how would somebody from ... solve your problem?

   This idea is written on a post-it. Try to come up with 2 or 3 ideas / function.

4. Repeat the same process for the other columns (industry, organisation, culture and random).

Example: you pick number 12 from column one: Aministration. Possible ideas could be: 'For one week, all emails from administration will start with a creative movie of 30 seconds before the real message becomes visible'. Column 2 - number 13: Pharmaceutical - 'We develop a pill that makes people more creative'. Column 5 - number 10: Harley biker - 'People who come up with a great idea get a temporary tattoo with the message 'I am a very creative person' ...

5. TRENDS SOCIETY

1. A group of max 8 people gather around a table and one person has a piece of paper and will write
2. Everybody can add a trend in society and the writer creates a mindmap with all suggestions (go as broad as possible in terms of trends - don't stick to your own industry) - 3 minutes to get as many associations as possible
3. Put mindmap in the middle & divide group in pairs. Every pair picks an association that has nothing to do with original question
4. Use that trend as inspiration to generate new ideas. Switch trend after 2 or 3 ideas.

Example: you pick the trend 'globalisation'. Possible ideas: 'Take 10 minutes to do a google search on how other companies are stimulating creativity.' or 'let employees who come back from a holiday share some innovations or bizarre things they have learned abroad.' Trend 'Artificial Intelligence'. Possible ideas: 'All employees get an AI chip to generate more ideas.' or 'Invite a trend-watcher for a speech.'

6. SUPERHERO

1. Groups of 4 people and everybody shares his or her hero (could be a real or fictive person, comics, historical figures, ...).
2. Choose the hero that everybody recognises but not a stereotypical hero like Superman
3. Write down some charactericstics of that hero
4. How would the hero solve your problem? Use the different characteristics to come up with different ideas
5. Re-associate - translate the actions of the hero into concrete solutions

Example: you pick Frodo from Lord of the Rings as your hero. Characteristics: small, courage, no special heroic powers, ring, accompanied by his friend Sam. Then you reframe the question: What would Frodo do to stimulate more creativity? Possible ideas: 'Go on a quest to find the solution.' Or 'Organise a quest within the company where employees have to bring in ideas to solve the quest.' 'Ask for help from friends' could lead to 'Every employee will contact a friend in a different organisation and ask what kind of initiatives they take to stimulate creativity.'

LOOKING FOR MORE?

Then I can suggest to have a look at the 27 methods shared by Marc Heleven and Ramon Vullings

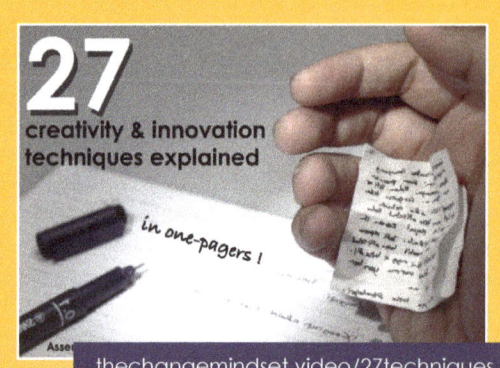

27 creativity & innovation techniques explained

in one-pagers !

thechangemindset.video/27techniques

"CREATIVITY IS ONE OF THE LAST REMAINING LEGAL WAYS OF GAINING AN UNFAIR ADVANTAGE OVER THE COMPETITION."

ED MC CABE

7. REVERSE THINKING

1. Reverse the question

   In this case: 'How can I make sure that nobody in my team will come up with new ideas?'

2. Invent ideas for the new problem statement on a seperate sheet

3. Reverse every idea on the list and re-associate. Go to the extremes - don't just reverse the negative idea into a positive one. How would the extreme positive side look like, + also explore if you can stay on the negative side and turn that into something positive.

Example: a 'negative' idea could be: 'If you have an idea, you have to fill out 7 documents and get 4 signatures before you can share it'. If you reverse this idea, you could get the following 'real ideas': 'Create a very easy process to share ideas - in every meeting we allocate 10 minutes for new ideas', or you stay on the negative side 'You have to follow a difficult process to make sure that you are really motivated to share that idea.' or 'Make it very exclusive - only the top 10% of the best employees can come up with new ideas'.

ACT

Suspending your judgement and switching perspectives to generate new ideas are two crucial ingredients of the change mindset. That being said, their value diminishes quickly if you don't add the third ingredient: action. Your plan will always be different than reality.

BaNano-actions are very small steps that you take to see if you're going in the right direction. Sometimes things go wrong, so I'll introduce you to a new word 'the nearling' which will help you to adapt a 'fail fast, forward and often' attitude to increase your success-rate.

PLAN ≠ REALITY

Planning is a crucial element for every project. Without a plan or direction, we will allow chaos to take over. However, it looks like the balance has shifted to the opposite side of the spectrum. In many companies, planning has become more important than the action itself. Employees spend months on analysing and developing the perfect plan, but once the plan is 'confronted' with the reality outside the meeting room, it shatters into pieces in a very short time.

A project is a living, growing process and won't happen in a vacuum. No matter how much time you spend planning, something will change, and if that makes large portions of your documentation obsolete, it means you have spent too much time creating it. Starting to act earlier on (with smaller actions) is often the best way to learn whether your plan is going in the right direction.

4 MONTHS WORKING ON THE BUDGET PLAN

In September every year, a team of several people begin working on the yearly budget for the next year. That process last for 4 months, and takes up a lot of the resources and time of our people. Nobody will argue that it's bad to have a good plan ready, but the reality shows that the plan already has to be adapted drastically after 4 weeks into the new year, because the conditions and environment change really quickly in our industry. Now it looks like nobody is referring to the budget plan anymore - until it gets back on the agenda in September of next year.

Manager large telecommunication provider

PLAN

REALITY

"IF PLAN 'A' FAILS, REMEMBER YOU HAVE 25 LETTERS LEFT."

CHRIS GUILLEBEAU

BUT HOW CAN YOU GET BACK ON TRACK WHEN THINGS GO AWRY?

+ Be aware that this 'reality check' will happen. You will get distracted or change your mind so don't go into panic mode.

+ Reach out for support. Have a chat with a friend, coach or colleague to solicit empathetic support so you can move out of 'self-blaming' fast.

+ Come back to why you're doing what you're doing in the first place. Connect to your mission again.

+ Pay attention to what's true. Make a distinction between what's really true and your excuses to avoid a certain fear.

+ Recalibrate. It's time to get back on track. Take out your plan, adjust accordingly – however big or small – and get moving again. Your work matters. Your business matters too.

THE BANANO ACTION

More and more companies offer their employees a piece of fresh fruit as a healthy perk. Often, you'll notice that the bananas are gone, and the oranges are still there. How is this possible? It's not that bananas are objectively more delicious than oranges. The difference in their popularity comes down to one thing: how easy are they to peel.

Tania Luna & Jordan Cohen have done research on this topic and call this phenomenon the 'banana principle'. Human beings operate on the principle of the Least Effort - given several paths, we choose the easiest. How can we reduce friction so that positive actions feel more like a glide than an uphill trek? We can use this banana-principle to support all kind of change initiatives. How can we reduce friction if we want our employees to behave in a certain way?

Make the change as easy as possible. For example, do you want more brainstorming in your offices? Then make sure people have access to post-its and flipcharts in every room. You want people to switch off the lights when they go home? Put the garbage bin under the light switch because there's a good chance that people want to throw something away before they go home.

Positive psychologist Shawn Achor talks about the 20 second rule. He believes that 20 seconds can make all the difference when it comes to behavior change. Specifically, making tasks slightly easier or more accessible will encourage you to do them, whereas making a behavior slightly harder will decrease the likelihood that you will give in to your urges. If something – such as checking your social media – takes you 20 seconds longer to do, you're less likely to do it.

A BaNaNo action is the first, small step that you can take to check if an idea or project has potential. Imagine that you have a limited amount of money (max. 10 euro/dollar) & time (max. 1 hour)

BANANO ACTION: OLD REPORTS

At a larger financial organisation in Belgium, I had the opportunity to collaborate with a team responsible for delivering monthly reports with key figures for 9 other departments. Every month these departments receive an extensive report with key figures of the previous month. I call them the 'Report Team'. They felt that nobody was really reading these reports, although they were time consuming to create.

The Report Team decided to change the extensive paper report into a short digital summary, with only key figures that the specific departments needed. Due to egos and political games, they knew that the department's heads wouldn't agree to this. Consequently, the report team decided that they would experiment with a 'BaNaNo-action'.

The following month, they resent out an 'old' report (from 2 months earlier) to one department, only changing the title and announced it as the most recent report available. Nothing happened. The next month, they sent out the exact same 'old report' to all departments. None but one department noticed the mistake. This proved the Report Team's hypothesis that hardly anyone paid attention to their reports.

THE PIANO STAIRS

'The piano stairs' is an initiative from the funtheory.com. The stairs will play notes of a melody or piano tones when people walk on them. These artworks stimulate people to take the stairs instead of the elevator or escalator.

thechangemindset.video/piano-stairs

This encouraged the Report Team to organise a meeting with the department's heads, announcing that they would only receive a digital summary in the future. As expected, they were annoyed, claiming they needed the extensive report.

Thanks to the BaNaNo actions, they could prove that people weren't reading the reports. The heads conceded to smaller digital report, saving a lot of time and money for the Report Team as well as giving them the satisfaction of actually having made an impact on a change that in future allowed them to focus on more important tasks.

CHANGE BEHAVIOR GROUP

DR. MATTHIJS VAN LEEUWEN AND PROF. DR. RICK VAN BAAREN - BEHAVIOR CHANGE GROUP, FIRST MASTER AROUND BEHAVIOUR CHANGE, TEACHING, SPEAKING, INSPIRING, REBELS, FUN, ...

A PSYCHOLOGICAL LANDSCAPE

A change project should always start with defining a clear end goal. What is the behaviour that you want to achieve (for yourself, or your team)? The next step is creating a psychological landscape of the steps that are needed to get there. What are the motivators? What may block that behaviour? What kind of context do we need to create to make sure that the desired behaviour will stick? What is the psychology behind the current behaviour?

People can, of course be motivated or blocked by different causes, depending on their life story. Once you have a better view of this 'landschape', you can choose an approach to take steps in changing that behaviour.

CROSS-INDUSTRY LEARNING

Both behavioural scientist are also spending quite some time in exploring different domains to broaden their own knowledge and experience. At this moment, they are exploring the domain of brain science and clinical psychology to find new insights on how this can be applied in their business.

What can you learn from a different domain in your business?

NUDGING OR INTRINSIC MOTIVATION

Nudges are small changes in the environment that are easy and inexpensive to implement. The urinal fly is a nice example: by having images of flies etched near the drains of the bathroom urinals, spillage on the bathroom floor was reduced by 80%. So, nudging is an easy way to steer the behaviour of people in a certain direction, and can also certainly be used in the short term.

However, in the long run people get used to these 'tricks'. Intrinsic motivation is a lot stronger, because people make a more conscious choice to adapt certain behaviours in line with their values and goals. If you want to change behaviour in the long run, make sure you pay attention to both methods.

BRUSHING TEETH IN NEPAL

A group of dentists were visiting Nepal every year to fix children's teeth. They combined this with some prevention campaigns in schools, and created leaflets to make children aware that brushing teeth was important. However, they discovered that their campaign didn't have a lot of success because during the rest of the year, most children didn't make the effort to brush their teeth.

At one point, they switched their strategy: instead of educating the children, they asked them 2 questions: 1. What is your dream? What do you want to become in life? 2. Why do you think it's important to have healthy teeth?

The children shared their answers in the group. Then, they were asked to show the dentists how you should brush your teeth. The crucial moment happened at the end of the session where they asked the kids why they asked those 2 questions at the start. At that moment, the children made a connection between the two questions- If I want to realize my dream, I need to take care of my teeth. This connection led to a more sustainable change in behaviour, because they were now motivated on an intrinsic level.

CHANGING BEHAVIOUR

There are three important elements that have an influence on behaviour:

+ Physical and mental capacities: are you able to fulfill the activity? If you want to run a marathon, then it helps if you are in good condition and train a lot.
+ Motivation: you have a desire to do the activity. There is a distinction between conscious motivation and unconscious motivation (our fixed patterns to do certain activities)
+ Physical and social environment: are you in the right (physical and social) space to perform certain activities?

These three elements are interrelated, and influence each other. For example: if your physical shape is is bad, it will be harder to motivate yourself to start every day with a run. A sunny day, (for instance when you see a lot of people run in your neighbourhood) will also influence your own motivation. It's important to keep those three factors in mind if you want to change your own behaviour or the behaviour of others.

Reasons why it is so hard to change behaviour:

+ Automatic behaviour wins most of the time (because you do it unconsciously). It seems almost impossible to change your leadership style or quit smoking after 15 years. Repeating and rewarding the new behaviour often is a good way to start changing.
+ Human beings prefer to avoid pain instead of gaining pleasure. Change usually requires a temporary loss or pain before you will feel the advantages of new behaviour.
+ Changing behaviour is closely connected to our social and physical environment. If we don't change our environment, there is a high risk that we'll stick to old habits.

Changing behaviour with BaNano actions:

+ Be specific about the desired change in behaviour (not the result)
+ Make it as easy as possible
+ Connect it to a trigger in your environment that you are already doing
+ Celebrate the small wins to stay motivated

*Small move, big change
by Caroline Arnold*

Micro resolutions

The reason why we fail to keep a resolution is due to our habits and routines. We spend a lot of our time on autopilot (because that saves mental energy), and that makes it quite hard to change our behaviour. If we want to get rid of a bad habit we have to make sure that we cultivate the opposite of how our autopilot is wired, and that means being fully aware of our actions. Caroline Arnold calls these small actions a micro-resolution in her book Small Move, Big Change. You would take your broad and unmanageable resolutions, chop them up and turn them into precise and practical steps that you can quickly achieve. Instead of saying 'I'm going to be more assertive', you could create a BaNano action- 'I'm going to ask at least one question in the next meeting'. You can immediately see the result of your resolution because after the meeting, you will know if you succeeded or not.

Make sure you ease into a process and don't overwhelm yourself with 10 BaNano actions at the same time, because each one by itself looks easy, even though you still have to do them. The smaller and easier the action, the higher the success rate.

Some tips for your BaNano actions:

+ Positive framing (I will write for 30 minutes every day on my book), or zero-tolerance framing (no computer or smart- phone after 9PM)
+ Connect the BaNano action to a recognizable cue in your environment (I will put my running shoes next to my bed before a run because they are the trigger for going for a 20 minute run the next morning).

Decisive
by Dan & Chip Heath

Dan & Chip Heath introduce in their book 'Decisive' the word 'Ooching'. It means using small experiments to test one's hypothesis. It is the opposite of jumping in headfirst into something. For example, taking an internship is a good idea because it's the fastest way to discover whether or not we want to pursue a certain profession. Is there an option to do some ooching before you commit 100% towards something?

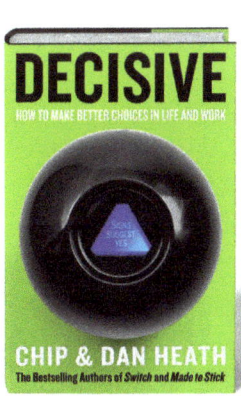

SHOW UP IN THE ARENA

"It is not the critic who counts; not the man who points out how the strong man stumbles, or where the doer of deeds could have done them better. The credit belongs to the man who is actually in the arena, whose face is marred by dust and sweat and blood; who strives valiantly; who errs, who comes short again and again, because there is no effort without error and short-coming; but who does actually strive to do the deeds; who knows great enthusiasms, the great devotions; who spends himself in a worthy cause; who at the best knows in the end the triumph of high achievement, and who at the worst, if he fails, at least fails while daring greatly, so that his place shall never be with those cold and timid souls who neither know victory nor defeat."

Theodore Roosevelt

JUMP IN AND SWIM

For the long term it's more interesting if not crucial to let graduates experiment with certain tasks and processes instead of giving them pre-defined action steps. Why not just let them experiment and learn by doing and allow failure. Instead of narrowing their creativity with rules and exact instructions. I present them the broader picture and let them discover ways to solve the challenge. And it has happened more often than not that my graduates come up with solutions that are more effective & time efficient than the way we have done it for years.

Manon de Boer - Partner Tax & Legal @ Deloitte

#BESOMEBODY

Besomebody Founder & CEO Kash Shaikh shares a powerful message on why it's not supposed to be easy. Everyone wants the prize, but nobody's willing to pay the price.

thechangemindset.video/be-somebody

#besomebody.

ASKING FOR FORGIVENESS INSTEAD OF PERMISSION

Many people spend a lot of time getting other people (mostly their boss) on board for a certain project. This requires time and energy, whilst the initiators are mainly busy with creating documents and business plans to prove that their project will have an impact.

Instead of spending different resources on developing these documents, it might be more interesting if they spend the time and resources on testing a BaNano action. If it's a success: congrats, because you have just achieved your first mini-business case in order to convince your peers and executives. If the BaNano action fails, ask for forgiveness, and share your learnings about the path that you have explored. You have learned more than somebody who spent that time on writing a plan.

Don't get me wrong; at certain times, it's a great idea to create a business plan and documents to share your vision and milestones. However, in the beginning of a new project, doing several small BaNano-actions will generate a better return on investment than spending that time writing theoretical plans.

"PERSEVERANCE IS STUBBORNNESS WITH A PURPOSE."

JOSH SHIPP

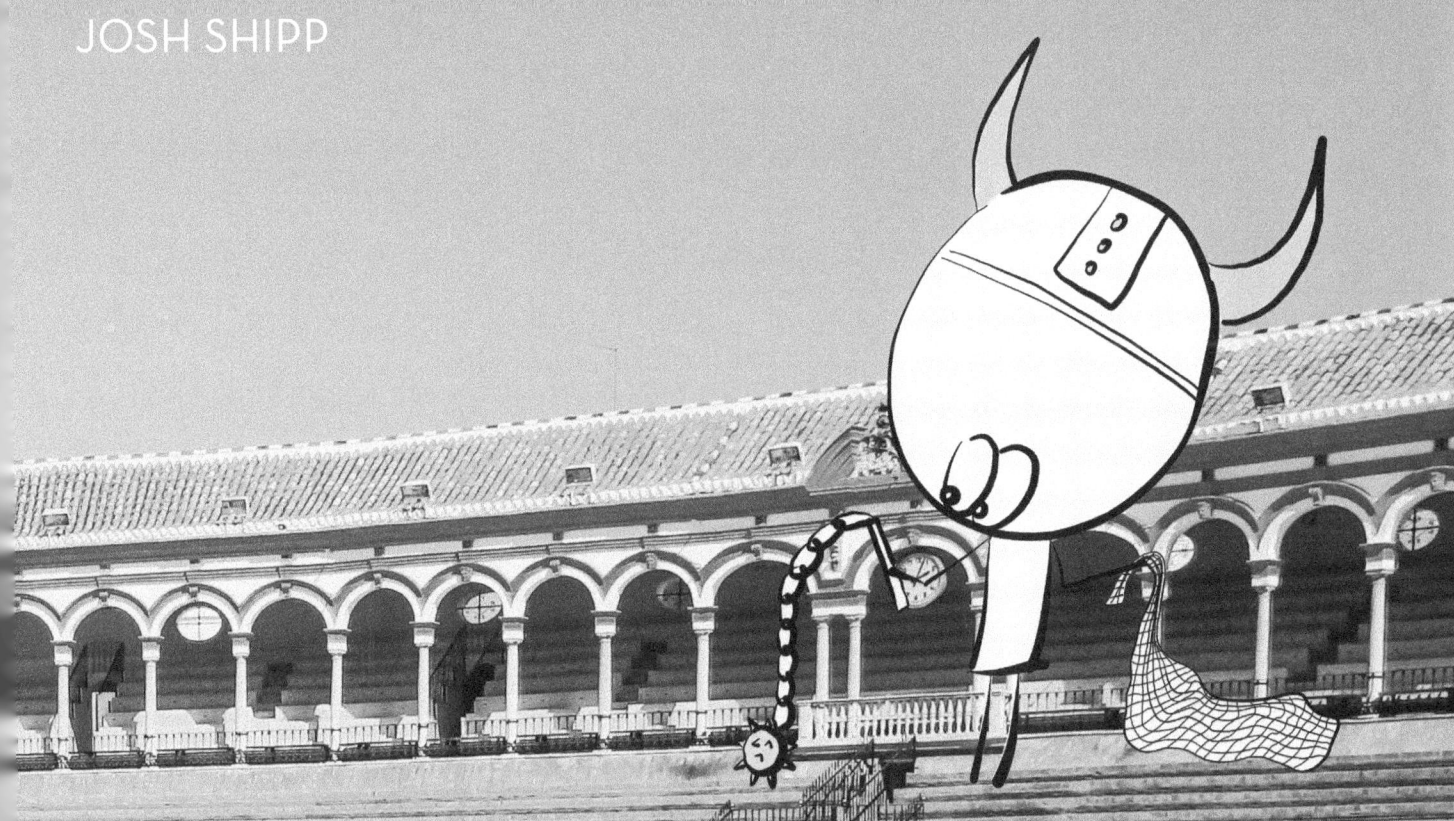

BREAKING THE PROCRASTINATION HABIT

Most of us are occasionally guilty of procrastinating. This is quite logical because we're juggling all the time with competing priorities which all require attention, time and energy. Sometimes procrastination can be a serious problem if we don't take action for the important parts in our career, relationships or physical health. Procrastination can become a habit that's hard to break.

Mel Robbins - author of The 5 Second Rule - has done a lot of research into the procrastination domain, and has found that we connect procrastination with being lazy or incompetent. In reality, procrastination is actually a behavioural pattern meant to help us cope with stress. What we are avoiding isn't the task itself but rather the stress that we are associating with the task.

So, procrastination is a coping mechanism to protect us from too much stress. Facebook and YouTube are great ways to release stress, and they give us the feeling that we're doing something safe instead of doing a 'dangerous' activity (which might cost attention, time and energy).

Other examples of recognizable and potentially stressful situations that we would easily try to postpone are working on preparing a public speech, or having a possible difficult conversation with your partner.
Mel came up with a very simple (I love it) method called the 5-Second Rule. There are two easy steps:

1. The very first thing to do is to acknowledge that you're stressed. Don't analyse it, just accept it.

2. Make a five-second decision that is directly contrary to the stress response. Count backwards from 5 to 1, and take action. It's the power of a (small) push.

This is a decision of courage, because instead of letting your slow brain come in and start analyzing the situation, you take the decision - within 5 seconds - to spend a few minutes confronting the element that you're fearful of doing. If it's a phone call, just pick up the phone and call. It could be writing, where you decide in those 5 seconds to start writing for the next 5 minutes, no matter what comes out. The result of the action isn't that important, what really counts is that you broke the habit of procrastination and proved that you can confront the stress.

Decide and act.

It sounds like a very simple method but doing it requires of course the guts to scrutinizingly see your behaviour for what it is (fear of stress and action), and setting out to change your behaviour. It may take time, but give it a try. There's a good chance that while you're reading this bookazine you might have something else to do. Maybe unconsciously, you're procrastinating right now. Think about it. 5 ... 4 ... 3... 2... 1 and take that first action!

Still reading ... Mmmm ;-)

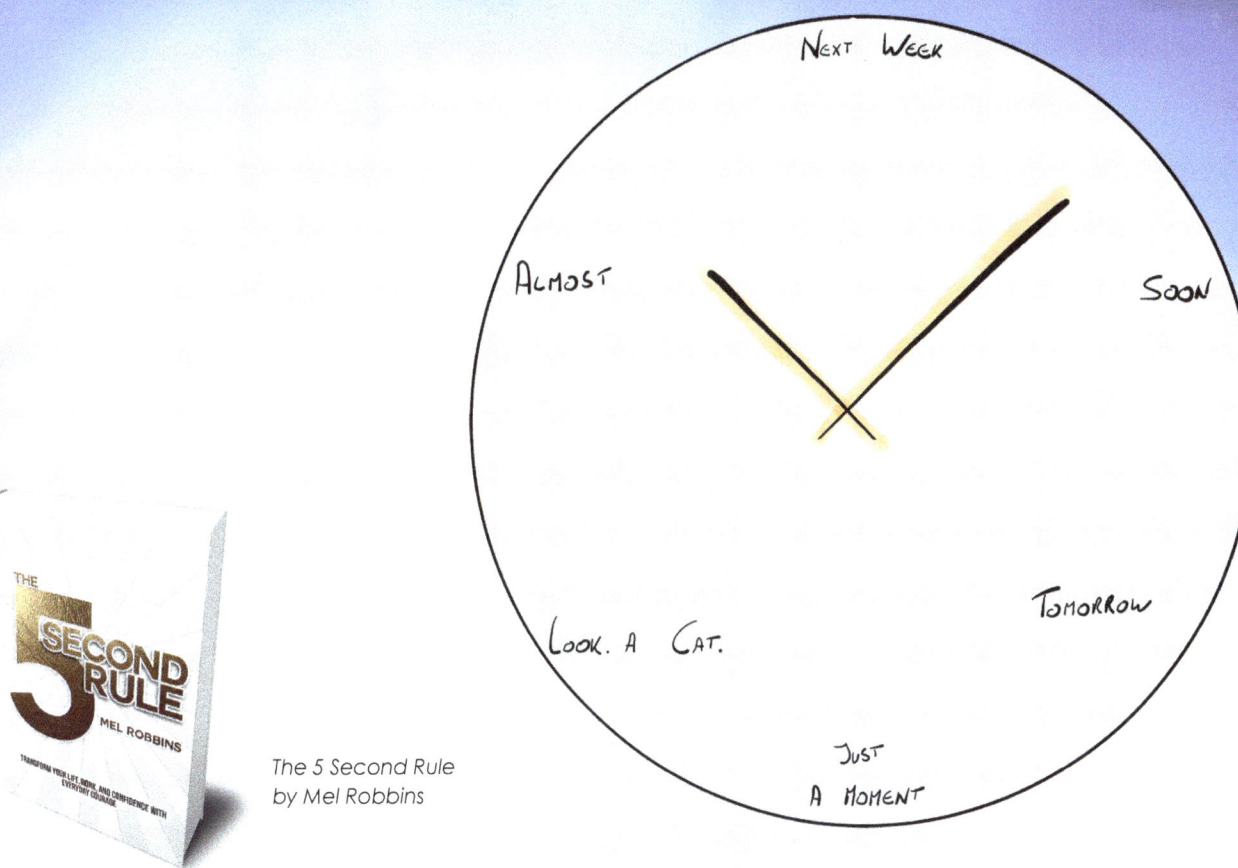

The 5 Second Rule
by Mel Robbins

Show the disadvantages of the status quo

We human beings need a certain degree of dissatisfaction and insecurity in order to change. If we would be happy all the time then we probably would still be cavemen because there would be no need for change. The fact that we are unhappy with a certain situation drives us to go out of our comfort zone and explore innovative ways and change possibilities.

That is one of the reasons why it is really important to show people - almost confront them - with the negative aspects of the status quo during a change project. Quite often we only talk about the advantages of the new situation but we don't pay a lot of attention to the current situation. In the same way we find it self-evident to calculate the cost of a change initiative but we forget to balance that against the potential cost of not moving forward.

Staying put in a status quo and finally lagging behind will eventually cost you in losing customers to the competition or in fines for not meeting new regulations for instance.

There always is a very real cost to not changing at all. If you want to engage people in a change process, they need to feel some discomfort in the current situation. Why should I otherwise leave my comfort zone (which is real) and take a lot of risks for an (imaginary) better future.

"Tomorrow is often the busiest day of the week."
Spanish proverb

WHAT I LEARNED FROM 100 DAYS OF REJECTION

Jia Jiang adventures boldly into a territory so many of us fear: rejection. By seeking out rejection for 100 days -- from asking a stranger to borrow $100 to requesting a "burger refill" at a restaurant -- Jiang desensitized himself to the pain and shame that rejection often brings and, in the process, discovered that simply asking for what you want can open up possibilities where you expect to find dead ends.

thechangemindset.video/100daysrejection

What I learned from 100 days of rejection

LEARNING FROM FAILURE

International aid groups make the same mistakes over and over again. David Damberger analyzes his own engineering failure in India -- and calls for his friends in the development sector to publicly admit, scrutinize and learn from their missteps.

What happens when an NGO admits failure

thechangemindset.video/learning-failure

THE UNEXPECTED BENEFIT OF CELEBRATING FAILURE

Th"Great dreams aren't just visions," says Astro Teller. "They're visions coupled to strategies to make them real." The head of X (formerly Google X), Teller takes us inside the "moonshot factory", where his team seek to solve the world's biggest problems through experimental projects like balloon-powered Internet and wind turbines that sail through the air. They have found a way to balance the paradox of enthusiastic skepticism and boundless optimism to comfortably work on big, risky projects and explore audacious ideas

thechangemindset.video/moonshotfactory

The unexpected benefit of celebrating failure

TED TALKS

SMART FAILURE FOR A FAST CHANGING WORLD

The world is changing much more rapidly than most people realize, says business educator Eddie Obeng -- and creative output cannot keep up. In this spirited talk, he highlights three important changes we should understand for better productivity, and calls for a stronger culture of "smart failure."

thechangemindset.video/smart-failure

Smart failure for a fast-changing world

SUCCESS, FAILURE AND THE DRIVE TO KEEP CREATING

Elizabeth Gilbert was once an "unpublished diner waitress," devastated by rejection letters. And yet, in the wake of the success of 'Eat, Pray, Love,' she found herself identifying strongly with her former self. With beautiful insight, Gilbert reflects on why success can be as disorienting as failure and offers a simple -- though hard -- way to carry on, regardless of outcomes.

Success, failure and the drive to keep creating

thechangemindset.video/success-failure

IT'S A NEARLING!

Mentally, we are used to focusing on error and failure prevention, when we should actually let go of this focus and start learning from our mistakes. For true innovation, the ability to let go is just as important as thinking of the new. Sometimes it's better to start doing something and discover you're on the wrong path (you learned what isn't the right path) instead of doing nothing- because then you have zero chance of learning anything. Yet the words 'failure' and 'mistake' still have a negative connotation to them.

Let me introduce a new word: the nearling. A nearling is a positive word for something new that was done with the right intentions, which has not (yet) led to the right result.

The reasons why nearlings don't succeed can be diverse: the circumstances have changed; a better option has been chosen; an error was made; fate decided otherwise; suddenly priorities altered, and so on. On a binary scale the nearling is situated between zero and one, between failure and success. You only recognise a nearling in retrospect.

You can be proud of nearlings, because:

- You started something and took initiative
- You may have moved others
- Maybe it led you to something that was successful
- You need many nearlings, for a few successes
- You learned from it

The nearling emphasises that initiatives are almost always valuable, even if they don't lead immediately to the desired result. They may be the result of an experiment gone awry, or of something unexpected, yet something has been learned from it.

Check out many examples on nearling.com

YOU NEED NEARLINGS TO CREATE LEARNINGS

We apply the 'nearling' principle already in different situations. Take the situation where a kid is learning to ride a bike. At a certain moment, there's a good chance that the kid will fall.

Have you ever seen a parent that starts to scold their child when falling because it failed? Have you often seen the kid blaming the bike, the bumpy road, the strong wind coming from the East, … well, actually they do sometimes.

The parent usually re-assures the child that falling is part of the learning process and - with a kiss on the knee - the child jumps on the bike again and starts over. That's the nearling spirit. You tried something with the best intentions, but the result was different than expected. Learn from it and start over. Wouldn't it be great if we could apply the same energy in a business context? From nearling to learning, the anagram is not a coincidence.

A few of my personal nearlings & learnings

- Nearling: The first edition of my previous book. The format was just 3 millimeters too thick to fit in a normal envelope, and I had to use a postal package instead-which cost a lot more.
  Learning: For this book, I've decided to use a standard magazine format.

- Nearling: With a colleague, I printed 1000 business cards to promote a certain project (we even had a photoshoot done especially for it), but only distributed 5 of them because we came to the conclusion that this side-project wasn't working.
  Learning: for my future projects, I'll try them out first for a few months, and only then make a conscious decision whether or not it requires special promotion tools.

- Nearling: I had to give a speech for a group of volunteers, but I didn't inquire about out their age. It appeared that the average age was 70. It forced me to improvise and translate my 'examples' into their world view to get my message across.
  Learning: my briefing meetings with the client are now a lot better prepared after that incident.

- Nearling: my previous girlfriends.
  Learning: they helped me to grow as a person and resulted in finding a woman I completely love and knowing how to love her (or at least have a well-intended shot at it :).

What are your nearlings & learnings of the last year?

DEVELOP A NEARLING CULTURE

You will find several examples how you can create a culture in your organisation that allows space to talk about nearlings and stimulate a more entreprenerial mindset.

The nearling circle

Gather in a special place designed for a weekly or monthly nearling ceremony.
Invite the people to stand up (one at a time), and confess a mistake or nearling in front of the crowd.

Let them answer the following 3 questions:

- What did you fail at?
- How did you cope with it?
- What would you do differently?

Celebrate the mistake with a round of applause, or preferably with beer and champagne.

Do's

- Encourage the most senior leader in the room to admit his or her nearling to start with.
- Make sure you create a truly safe environment. If at any time any sanctions are made, trust will vanish instantly.
- Create a prize for the best nearling.

Don'ts

- No blaming and shaming.
- Do not expect that everyone wants to share their biggest nearlings from the start. Normally, people find it very discomforting to genuinely open up. Don't force it, be patient and keep building trust.
- If people repeat the same mistake over and over again, something is wrong. When this happens, it means they are not learning from previous mistakes.

'Failure is not an option. It's a privilige

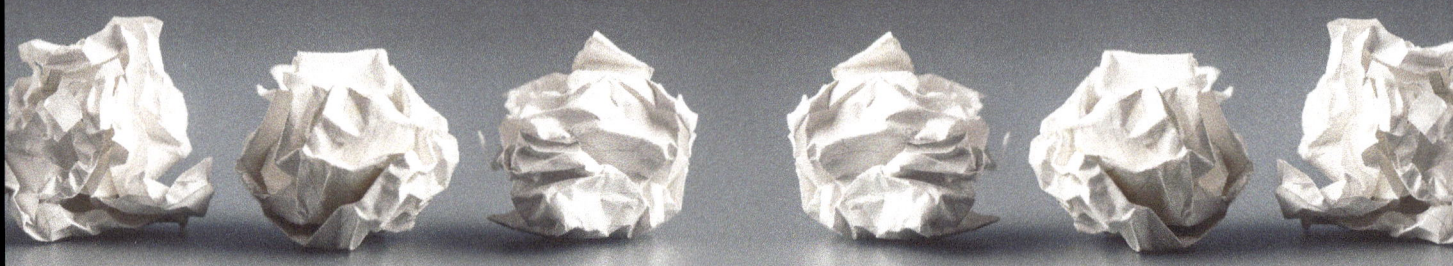

Add KPIs to reward risk and failure

Most KPIs are tied exclusively to productivity, efficiency and boosting the bottom line. However, without incentivizing risk taking and without making allowances for the inevitable outcomes that comes with taking risks (failure), innovation will remain all talk and no action. To truly make trying new things part of the culture, employees must be measured by it. A simple way of doing this is to hold employees accountable for trying a new approach to one of their tasks each quarter.

FuckUp Nights

Fuckup Nights is a global movement to share stories of business and professional failure. It is powered by an event series in 250 cities of 80 countries. Since it began a few years ago, the initiators of the FuckUp Nights have started a research arm called 'the Failure Institute', to do research on all the cases shared at the Fuckup Nights to help decision makers make better decisions.

Oeps, we forgot the most important value

To make sure that everybody in our company would understand the core values, we took several actions. We started with checking if our 'old' values still represent the 'new' company that we want to be and did several sessions with the senior leadership team to identify our 'new' core values. After that, we had (town hall meetings) WORK SHOPS with ALL our employees to start discussions about these values and what they would mean in our daily business processes. And we had to make some hard decisions to say goodbye to some leaders who didn't fit in our 'new' organisation anymore.

Another idea to spread the message, was creating a note block with the core values on it & every employee would recieve one of those note blocks. It turned out we missed the most important one, Safety! We had taken that value so for granted, that we actually forgot to explicitly notice it on the block.

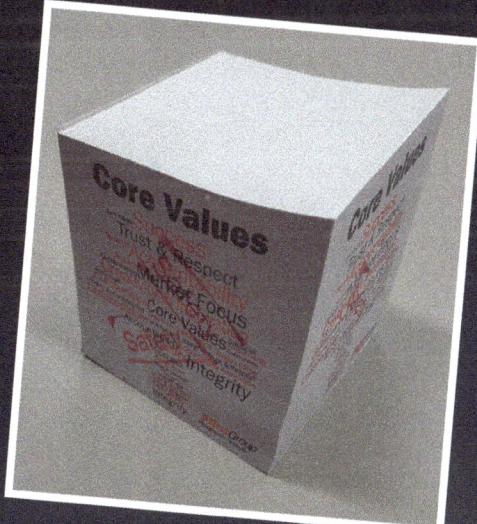

Instead of considering this as a big failure, we looked at it from the point of a nearling - we did something with the right intention but it didn't work out as expected. And that mindset helped us to use this nearling as an opportunity to emphasize the importance of Safety even more. We gave everyone a stamp with the word Safety on and asked them to stamp it on the note block themselves. It turned out that it was a great way to make sure that Safety is in the heads of all our people.

HR Director @ large supplier to printing and packaging industry

rved only for those who try.' - Anonymous

THE CORPORATE REBELS ARE ON A MISSION TO MAKE WORK MORE FUN. THEY QUIT THEIR FRUSTRATING, CORPORATE JOBS AND SET OUT TO TRAVEL THE GLOBE, VISITING THE WORLD'S MOST INSPIRING ORGANIZATIONS. WHILE CHECKING OFF THEIR RENOWNED BUCKET LIST, THEY SHARE EVERYTHING THEY LEARN. THEIR BLOGS ARE READ BY 50 000 PEOPLE EVERY MONTH, AND THE GROUP HAS AN ACTIVE SLACK COMMUNITY OF 2000 PEOPLE WORLDWIDE WHO KEEP THE CONVERSATIONS GOING.

CREATE A PLAYGROUND

Creating a more exciting workplace is of course attractive, but it means changing the current situation, and a lot of people associate change with fear. They have to behave differently, take more responsibility and accept the fear of the unknown. For that reason, create a playground, or context where people can experiment with small changes in a safe environment. Give them the freedom to take decisions within certain limits, and discuss the results and the process. It's very important that the borders of the playground are transparent for everybody. Show people the positive and negative results and then evaluate how you can improve.

CORPORATE REBELS

EVERY COMPANY CAN MAKE THE CHANGE

One of the great insights they have is that you don't have to go to the famous companies like Google, Spotify or Semco. You can find very engaged employees, and totally new ways of working everywhere. An example is Morning Star-it's the largest tomato processor in the world. The whole company is entirely self-managing: no bosses, no titles and no structural hierarchy. Another example is the Belgian Federal Office of Social Affairs -you wouldn't expect this kind of approach in a government environment! Frank van Massenhove leads that department, and he started by introducing new technologies which make it easy to work paperless and from home. Performance is only measured by results-employees decide the process and number of working hours. Within the department, some people have the 'formal' task of challenging the status quo by asking how employees can improve the way they work.

GETTING COMMITMENT IS CRUCIAL

It all starts with a clear vision, and maximizing shareholder value (or profit) shouldn't be the only reason. Of course, we need profits but it's not the reason why organisations exist. An inspiring purpose, combined with a clear set of core values provides employees with lots of energy and motivation as well as direction. A crucial element is asking for a commitment from the workforce to go in a certain (new) direction. Most organizational transformations fail due to lack of commitment from everybody in the workforce. Inspired by a company in Spain, the Corporate Rebels apply this voting process. If they collaborate with a new client, they start by delivering an interactive speech about the possibilities of their own future workplace. They explain a possible direction for a change movement and explain that the employees need to be in charge of the initiatives. Then, there's an anonymous voting process ('yes' or 'no' for change). If more than 70% voted 'yes' then the project starts, otherwise they say goodbye to the client because the workforce wasn't ready for the change.

THERE'S O
MOMENT T

My name is Cyriel Kortleven which translates literally to 'Short Life' in English. From the moment I was born, every single day upon citing my name, I've been reminded that we are granted a limited time on this earth. This is the one absolute certainty we have in life: we are born at a certain moment and we will die. A lot of people approach this fact in a very heavy way and feel a bit sad about it. They are hoping that some day the 'elixir of Eternal Life' will be invented. However you can also look at this fact from a different perspective. Today is a new day and you can decide to live your life to the fullest, today.

I believe that you can choose to change your mindset at this very moment. Results won't be instantly visible. They may even ask a lot of effort and endurance but it sure starts with a decision; the decision to make a change. Are you committed to decide to start doing things in a different way? Are you committed to make sacrifices to go in a certain direction? Are you committed to go out of your comfort zone – even out-of-your-box - and do the hard work of changing your life?

CHANGE HAPPENS  NOW

LY ONE

O CHANGE

A BIG THANK YOU TO ...

Despite the fact that I'm a man, I hope that I may compare the writing of a book with a pregnancy. I would even dare to say that writing this bookazine felt like a double pregnancy. I have put a lot of time, energy and love in this creation for the last 18 months. And I'm very happy with my newborn.

But like every big and successful project, I couldn't have done this on my own.

Kathleen Steegmans - the graphic designer - for the beautiful design of the bookazine. We have spent many hours and exchanged truckloads of emails playing around with the concept and fine-tuning the design. The result looks very beautiful and inspiring.

Katrien De Cannière for being a sparring partner; a proofreader and for structuring and editing all my content inventions. And to David Esterhuysen for an extra layer of text editing. The two of you made sure that readers can actually read the bookazine.

Dirk de Jong for supporting my research, preparing the interviews and having chats and calls that helped turning this book into a success.

My friends and colleagues within 21 Lobsterstreet for your support in many shapes and forms: Igor Byttebier, Johan D'Haeseleer, Joost Kadijk, Karen Van Heuckelom, Marc Heleven, Martine Vanremoortele, Ramon Vullings & Willem Stortelder.

All the people that I've interviewed for their time and willingness to share their insights: Angelo Vermeulen, Brady Pyle, Chris Bartlett, Christine Viklund, Eduardo Briceño, Frank De Winne, Freek-Jan Ronner, Harm Jans, John de Koning, Manon de Boer, Matthijs van Leeuwen, Reza Moussavian, Rick van Baaren, Rob Lilwall, Xavier Maassen, Zoltan Szeni.

Everyone in my network who supported me in his or her own way. By commenting on my questions and posts; filling out my questionnaire; sharing your personal and professional examples after a keynote; ...

The woman who answered 'Yes' to the most important question I ever dared to ask, Liane. Thanks for coming with me on this journey. You have helped me innumerable times by listening to my bizarre concepts and ideas, sending me motivating texts and pushing me to finish this book. I love you.

And last but not least, thank you for buying and reading the bookazine. I hope that I've inspired you with some new tools, language and energy to boost your Change Mindset. Spread the word.

Cyriel Kortleven

ABOUT THE AUTHOR

Imagine a man coming in. He's friendly. Joyful. Expressive. Very present to what you want to discuss with him and happy to be of service. His enthusiasm is contagious, his playfulness apparent, his creativity endless. At the same time he is practical and to the point. He knows his stuff. There's also something you can't quite put your finger on. A kind of innocence that puts you at ease. An openness that is integer and authentic. Take a deep breath, relax and allow that smile to emerge on your face ...

You've just met **Cyriel Kortleven**.

Cyriel is the first Belgian CSP (Certified Speaking Professional) and one of only 35 Global Speaking Fellows. But more importantly, Cyriel is on a mission: boosting the creative & entrepreneurial mindset of professionals in change. To that effect I deliver keynotes all over the world and write books around 'The Change Mindset'.

Are you looking for an inspiring keynote speaker in the area Change? Do you want your audience to leave your event energized and ready for real action? Are the words 'interactive', 'inspiring', 'fun', 'pragmatic tools and tips' and 'lots of energy' resonating with your event goals? Then dive into this bookazine for a quick overview and invite Cyriel as a keynote speaker at one of your events to achieve your goal.

'Cyriel' in 25 words: global speaker, author, Change Mindset, inspirator, Certified Speaking Professional (CSP), digital nomad, interaction, less is beautiful, Yes And Act, obstacle run, burning man, loves Liane, present.

www.cyrielkortleven.com - cyriel@cyrielkortleven.com - @CyrielKortleven

LESS IS BEAUTIFUL

Get inspired by stories from various organisations that have implemented the 'Less is Beautiful' philosophy.

Less is Beautiful is based upon 4 pillars:

+ Why more is too much
+ Start to stop
+ Simplify
+ Letting go

This book is written for professionals who operate in business and/or governments and who are looking for ways to gain more results with less effort. You will find a broad spectrum of tools & examples ranging from famous companies such as Google and Apple, which are known for their simple principles, to an unusual social media campaign from Harry Potter's theme park; or going from the NYC 311 call center to patient-centered hospitals; or tools like the Aunt Bertha test to totally new concepts like nearling or wonder walk.

www.lessisbeautiful.com

* This book is also available in Dutch: Meer met Minder

OTHER BOOKS BY
CYRIEL KORTLEVEN

TIMESPIRATION

This is a book about Time.
It's not a book about time-management.
It's not a book about the clock.
It's a book about Time and the different perspectives on this topic.

An inspiration source full of images, quotes, nice-to-know, poems and exercises to look from a different perspective to the concept Time.

www.timespiration.com

SOURCES OF INSPIRATION

BOOKS

- Abundance, by Peter Diamandis and Steven Kotler, 2014
- Born for this, by Chris Guillebeau, 2016
- Built to last, by Jim Collins and Jerry Porras, 2004
- Corporate Entrepreneurship, by Paul Burns, 2008
- Corporate Rebels. Making work more fun, by Joost Minnaar, Pim de Morree, Freek-Jan Ronner, 2018
- Creativity in Business, Igor Byttebier and Ramon Vullings, 2015
- Creativity Inc., by Ed Catmull and Amy Wallace, 2014
- Cycling home from Siberia, by Rob Lilwall, 2011
- De Ladder, by Ben Tiggelaar, 2018
- Decisive, by Dan and Chip Heath, 2013
- Fail fast, Fail often, by Ryan Babineaux and John Krumboltz, 2013
- Feel the Fear and Do it Anyway, by Susann Jeffers, 2017
- Good to Great, by Jim Collins, 2001
- How Google Works, by Eric Schmidt and Jonathan Rosenberg, 2017
- Improvisation Inc, by Robert Lowe, 2000
- Jump! - Deliver astonishing results by unleashing your leadership team, by Chris Henderson, 2017
- Lean Change Management, by Jason Little, 2014
- Less is Beautiful, Cyriel Kortleven, 2016
- Loswerken, by Jan Wolter Bijleveld and Ingeborg Deana, 2014
- Managing the Dynamics of Change, by Jerald Jellison, 2006
- Mindset, by Carol Dweck, 2007
- Mini Habits: smaller habits, bigger results, by Stephen Guise, 2013
- Momentum, by Michael McQueen, 2016
- Naar een nieuwe mindset, by Lut Wyers, 2015
- Not Invented here: Cross Industry Innovation, by Ramon Vullings and Marc Heleven, 2016
- Small Move, Big Change, by Caroline Arnold, 2014
- Steal like an Artist, by Austin Kleon, 2012
- Switch: How to change things when Change is hard, by Dan & Chip Heath, 2010
- Surprise: Embrace the Unpredictable and Engineer the Unexpected, by Tania Luna & LeeAnn Renninger, 2015
- The 5 second rule, by Mel Robbins, 2017
- The Agility Shift, by Pamela Meyer, 2015
- The Day after Tomorrow, peter Hinssen, 2017
- The Icarus Deception, by Seth Godin, 2012
- The Innovation Expedition, by Gijs van Wulfen, 2013
- The Lean Startup, by Eric Ries, 2011

- The Magic of Thinking Big, by David Schwartz, 2015
- The Management Shift, Vlatka Hlupic, 2014
- The Now Habit, Meil Fiore, 2007
- The Power of Habit, by Charles Duhigg, 2014
- The Small Big, by Steve Martin, Noah Goldstein and Robert Cialdini, 2014
- The Starfish and the Spider, by Ori Brafman and Rod Beckstrom, 2006
- The subtle art of not giving a F*ck, by Mark Manson, 2017
- Thinking, Fast and Slow, by Daniel Kahneman, 2013
- Timespiration, by Cyriel Kortleven, 2011
- Walking Home from Mongolia, Rob Lilwall, 2014
- Weird Ideas that Work, Robert Sutton, 2007
- What to do when it's your Turn, by Seth Godin, 2014
- Who killed Creativity, by Andrew Grant, 2012
- Work Rules, by Laszlo Bock, 2015
- Yes And - How to Go Big, Create Wealth, and Impact the World, by Kelly Leonard and Tom Yorton, 2015
- Yes And … Your Business, Gijs van Bilsen, Joost Kadijk and Cyriel Kortleven, 2013

GENERAL WEBSITES & BLOGS

- Behavior Change Group - www.gedragsverandering.nl
- Corporate Rebels - blog - www.corporate-rebels.com
- Fuckup Nights all over the world - www.fuckupnights.com
- HolacracyOne - www.holacracy.org/wp-content/uploads/2016/08/Holacracy-WhitePaper-v5.pdf
- Ideaboosters - www.ideaboosters.net
- Ideakillers - www.ideakillers.net
- Nearling - www.nearling.com
- The Failure Institute - www.thefailureinstitute.com
- Seth Godin - blog - www.seths.blog
- Nic Askew - soul biographies - www.soulbiographies.com

PICTURES

All pictures are bought from istockphoto.com, stock.adobe.com or shutterstock.com. If we got a picture from a different source then we have added the photo credits next to the picture. Or we have used my personal picturesw. All drawings are made by Cyriel Kortleven.

ARTICLES

- Alastair Dryburgh - Forbes - Persuasion: sometimes it's easier to change reality than people - 2016 - www.forbes.com/sites/alastairdryburgh/2016/05/21/persuasion-sometimes-its-easier-to-change-reality-than-people/#107f95c44389

- Andrew J. Oswald, Eugenio proto and daniel Sgroi - Department of Economics at the University of Warwick - Happiness and Productivity - 2014 - https://warwick.ac.uk/newsandevents/pressreleases/new_study_shows/

- Annabel Acton - Inc. - Celebrating Failure - 2017 - www.inc.com/annabel-acton/stop-talking-about-celebrating-failure-and-start-doing-it-with-these-4-ideas.html

- Chris Zook - Harvard Business Review - What stops companies from growing - 2017 - www.hbr.org/video/5652533451001/ whiteboard-session-what-stops-companies-from-growing

- Dan Pink - RSI Animate - Drive: The surprising truth about what motivates us - https://vimeo.com/15488784

- Harold L. Sirkin, Perry Keenan, and Alan Jackson - Harvard Business Review - The Hard Side of Change - 2005

- Gallup - worldwide employee study between 2011-2012 - https://news.gallup.com/poll/165269/worldwide-employees-engaged-work.aspx

- Gary Hamel - Harvard Business Review - Bureaucracy must Die - 2014

- IBM Global Study: Majority of organizational change projects fail - 2008 - https://www-03.ibm.com/press/us/en/pressrelease/25492.wss

- Jocelyn Campbell - 7 self-help myths that are keeping you stuck and effective brain-based strategies to use instead - www.farthertogo.com

- Josh Linkner - Inc dot com - The 7 sins of mediocrity - https://www.inc.com/josh-linkner/the-7-sins-of-mediocrity.html

- Marcia W. Blenko, Michael Mankins and Paul Rogers - Harvard Business Review - The decision-driven organization - 2010

- Mary Ellen Slayter - Monster - Jobs of the future - 2017 - www.monster.com/career-advice/article/cool-future-jobs

- Michal Addady - Fortune dot com - Being happy at work really makes you more productive - 2015 - http://fortune.com/2015/10/29/happy-productivity-work/

- Nat Berman - Money Inc - 10 future technology jobs that will exist in 10 years but don't now - 2016 - www.moneyinc.com/future-technology-jobs/

- Patty McCord - Harvard Business review - How netflix changed HR - 2014

- Rachel Hodin - Thoughtcatalog - ridiculous laws around the world - https://thoughtcatalog.com/rachel-hodin/2013/10/67-ridiculous-laws-from-around-the-world-that-still-actually-exist/

- Simon Sinek - 99U - Why leaders eat last - 2013 - https://youtu.be/ReRcHdeUG9Y

- Stephen G. Hasty Jr. - KPMG Global Transformation Study - Surviving in Disruptive Times - 2016

- Yves Morieux - Harvard Business Review - Smart Rules: six ways to get people to solve problems without you - 2011

MOVIES (& TED-TALKS)

- Ami Versano - Difference between single and double pendulum - https://youtu.be/AwT0k09w-jw

- Apple - perspective - https://youtu.be/TJ1SDXbij8Y

- Astro Teller - TED Talk - The unexpected benefit of celebrating failure - https://www.ted.com/talks/astro_teller_the_unexpected_benefit_of_celebrating_failure

- Barry Schwartz - TED Talk - The paradox of choice - https://www.ted.com/talks/barry_schwartz_on_the_paradox_of_choice

- Becel commercial - Stuck on an Escalator - https://youtu.be/47rQkTPWW2I

- BJ Fogg - TEDx Talk - Forget big change, start with a Tiny Habit - https://youtu.be/AdKUJxjn-R8

- Cyriel Kortleven - What's your perspective on life - https://youtu.be/H3dxsJJU3Mg

- David Damberger - TED Talk - What happens when an NGO admits failure - https://www.ted.com/talks/david_damberger_what_happens_when_an_ngo_admits_failure

- Eddie Obeng - TED Talk - Smart failure for a fast-changing world - https://www.ted.com/talks/eddie_obeng_smart_failure_for_a_fast_changing_world

- Elisabeth Gilbert - TED Talk - Success, failure and the drive to keep creating - https://www.ted.com/talks/elizabeth_gilbert_success_failure_and_the_drive_to_keep_creating

- Jia Jiang - TED Talk - What I learned from 100 days of rejection - https://www.ted.com/talks/jia_jiang_what_i_learned_from_100_days_of_rejection

- Joshua Weigel and Rebekah Weigel - The Butterfly Circus - http://thebutterflycircus.com/short-film/

- Kash Shaikh - Be Somebody - https://youtu.be/tt4jRorzyT4

- Killing good ideas may harm your future - https://youtu.be/K2xsHATZsTg

- Little Britain - Computer Says No - https://youtu.be/qNDS4kVwA68

- Marc Heleven & Ramon Vullings - 27 creativity & innovation techniques explained - https://www.slideshare.net/marcnewshoestoday/27-creativity-and-innovation-tools-in-onepagers

- Pepsi ad - with Shaolin Kungfu - https://youtu.be/h0l8wzv-4Gs

- Richard Wiseman - colour changing card trick - https://youtu.be/v3iPrBrGSJM

- Ruth Chang - TED Talk - How to make hard choices - https://www.ted.com/talks/ruth_chang_how_to_make_hard_choices

- Sheena Iyengar - TED Talk - The art of Choosing - https://www.ted.com/talks/sheena_iyengar_on_the_art_of_choosing

- TMB Bank - Make the difference - https://youtu.be/jU4oA3kkAWU

- The Guardian - Points of view - https://youtu.be/E3h-T3KQNxU

- The Fun Theory - paino stairs - https://youtu.be/2lXh2n0aPyw

"In a time when most people do not have time to read books authors need to be creative and that is just what Cyriel has been with this Bookazine. But to get read books need to be more than creative, they need to inspire - and that is much more difficult (trust me, I know as an author of ten books myself) but again Cyriel has done it. Cyriel is one of the most positive and inspiring people I know and in this Bookazine his positive and inspiring spirit shines through. If you can not get a one-on-one with Cyriel the second best thing is to get "the change mindset"."

- *Fredrik Haren, author of 'The Idea Book'.*

"Doing more of the same will get you to where you're heading but most likely not were you really want to be ... a constant change is needed to overcome that !! Cyriel's bookazine provides a set of refreshing and inspirational instruments that help driving transformation in all sorts of environments. A real survival guide."

- *Peter Lathouwers - Digital Innovation & Solutions Leader @ Cegeka*

"Whatever industry you work in, understanding and reacting to change is essential, to stay relevant and enable success."

- *Simon Yeowart, Program Director @ The Eventful Group*

"Having the tools to embrace change, creativity and action are absolutely necessary in these dynamic uncertain times. Cyriel has the unique ability to be both fun & profound in providing easy to get tools, processes and awareness creations that are completely relevant NOW! Whether you are a high flying executive, an entrepreneur or someone who wants to make a difference. Jump in to grow and expand your mind-set and abilities."

- *Mark Fraser-Grant, International Coach, Facilitator and Trainer @ Beyond Coaching*

"In this new world of Change, we constantly have to adapt and be more agile than before, otherwise we're left behind! Living in a VUCA world, means that we are confronted to situations or environments that stimulate high levels of Volatility, Uncertainty, Complexity and Ambiguity. In other words, it's crazy out there!. In his book, Cyriel manages to bring all of those concepts alive while giving tips and solutions in order to survive in it! Thanks for your visions & creativity Cyriel."

- *Michael Nielsen - Managing Director @ TENEO events*

"Having a Change Mindset is crucial in this age of disruption. Master storyteller and agent of change, Cyriel has written a transformative book that will impact your life and business. Start your change journey to prepare you for what is coming. Read this book!"

- *Jerome Joseph, CSP, Global Speaking Fellow, Global Speaker & Best Selling Author of 7 books on Branding*

"In my role as thoughtleader and speaker around customer-centric organisations, I see organisations struggle to keep up with all those changes in this high speed digital world. Cyriel's message around the Change Mindset is really a kind of survivalkit for those professionals in change. His bookazine is simple, pragmatic and very fun to read."

- *Steven Van Belleghem - author, keynote speaker and entrepreneur*

"Cyriel Kortleven's 'The Change Mindset' provides you with a cornucopia of ideas for surviving and thriving in a changing world. But beware...this book will make you re-think about your life and work and could lead to unexpected moments of happiness"!

- *James Taylor, MBA, FRSA, Keynote Speaker on Business Creativity, Innovation & Artificial Intelligence*

"Welcoming Change, even when it feels (very) uncomfortable, helps you to handle future change coming up. A lot of the tools & techniques in Cyriel's survivalkit are really useful and easy to apply. They have helped us to stimulate experimentation."
- *Sabine Blanchet, HR Director @ Unilever*

"Rarely do I read world class materials served up with strong practical application ideas. Cyriel Kortleven - thanks for a magnificent book. The visuals are amazing, the content life changing, and the results are showing up already."
- *Ian Stephens - Founder @ Enrich Training & Development*

"I am pleased with how easy it reads, you can browse back and forth, read 'an article', put it back, knowing that you will come back to it soon. It does read like a really good magazine which you always have lying around. In particular what I like best about the bookazine is that it's practical; it motivates and helps you to get into action; go change!"
- *Arjan Landesbergen - Director Customer Care EMEA @ Rockwell Automation*

"The world needs change like never before, which necessarily requires a change of mindset. Cyriel Kortleven's compelling contribution to this challenge is simple, yet powerful. By taking the time to intentionally suspend our judgment, assess situations from a fresh perspective, and then doing something different we might just reach the true potential of a human society that can live in balance with the natural systems we depend upon."
- *Simon Harvey, Executive Director @ Proxima Consulting*

"In The Change Mindset Cyriel provides actionable advice how to deal with change. With key insights cool examples & easy to apply tools, Cyriel helps you to take the next step up the ladder of change in organisations. This bookazine is suitable for both leaders & professionals searching for proven & tangible tools on how to deal with change in this ever more challenging world."
- *Ramon Vullings - international keynote speaker, cross-industry expert & ideaDJ @ RamonVullings.com*

"The secret to changing your mindset is simple. Get out of the way. And read this bookazine. And explore the mindsets of those who are already free and loving life. And then change your own mindset and your world. Cyriel Kortleven is The Change Mindset Guru and his latest bookazine offers us a treasure trove of ideas and advice for creating a truly extraordinary life."
- *John Hale, Global Keynote Speaker – The Strategic Mindset @ Hale Consulting Group*

"You can't change anything if you can't change your mind. Having a growth mindset is non-negotiable if you want anything great for your life and relationships. Cyriel has done amazing work to get so many useful tools and ideas into this beautifully illustrated "bookazine" - which I highly recommend."
- *Wynand Jacobs, Life and Relationship Coach @ The Identity Entity*

"A Change Mindset and a dare to try attitude are essential to become future-proof a in our continuously changing world"
- *Marleen Crombez, Innovation Coach @ Pfizer*

"The book hit me like a slice of lemon; fresh, provoking and edgy! If you share the mentality and mindset Cyriel puts through in the book you're in for a good and exciting future. If not, well.. it might just be exciting - Read it!
- *David JP Phillips, Coach, Public speaker & Founder @ SpeakerRating.com*

www.ingramcontent.com/pod-product-compliance
Lightning Source LLC
Chambersburg PA
CBHW041646120626
46547CB00018B/2627